big think

/noun/

removing mental blocks, challenging limitations,
and thinking beyond perceived barriers.

BIG THINK

BIG THINK

EMPOWERED THOUGHTS

LYNDSEY GETTY

THE THOUGHT METHOD CO.

To anyone who ever pretended a hairbrush was a microphone,

and in loving memory of Luke F. McLaughlin, III

—thank you for helping me think big.

The only limits you have are the limits you believe.
—Napoleon Hill

CONTENTS

THE BIG PICTURE

It may seem like Miley Cyrus performing a song at the Grammys, a podcaster known for making negative generalizations about women, and you reading this book have nothing in common. But you do. All three of you are dealing with mental blockers, just in different ways.

Miley is freeing herself from a belief many of us are taught in adolescence—that we need someone else's love to complete us.

The podcaster is building his platform (and likely his identity) on the limiting belief that gender determines a person's value or worth. (He just happens to be "lucky" enough to belong to the "superior" one.)

And you? Well, you're learning an important truth: limiting beliefs restrict your potential and narrow your worldview.

Here, we're pulling back the curtain. We'll break down the common, disempowering beliefs that keep us stuck, where they come from, how they affect us, and how to move forward in a more empowered direction. We'll talk about how to think big.

The first half of this book will help you identify and challenge the limiting beliefs (aka blockers) that have been holding you back. You'll see how these beliefs shape your worldview and how questioning them creates space for a bigger, more empowered mindset.

The second half introduces the Five Rules of Big Think. These rules will help you stay open to new ideas, expand your perspective, and take action toward a future that aligns with your true potential.

The rules are written as "I-ffirmations," which are affirmations that start with the word "I" and frame your goals as personal and achievable. By telling yourself, "I..." you create a powerful subconscious nudge to align your actions with your intentions.

The more you internalize these I-ffirmations, the more they'll shape your actions and strengthen your emotional clarity—and the faster you'll see results. As you read the rules, pay attention to which ones resonate with you most. Consider writing them down and repeating them when you wake up, throughout your day, or before bed.

Throughout the book, you'll find writing prompts to help you dig deeper into your own thoughts and beliefs. These prompts will encourage reflection and challenge your current mindset.

I wanted this to feel like a conversation, so while I've kept things to the point, I've also included notes and references in the back of the book if you'd like to explore further. For the best results, read this in the voice of a friend who genuinely wants you to succeed—because that's exactly how it was written, with your success in mind.

Before we begin, it's important to note that most resources on mental blockers focus on personal beliefs, like "I'm not good enough," or "I can't get the promotion."

While these are powerful, they don't tell the full story. Limiting beliefs also shape how we see the world and influence how we think about success, relationships, and opportunities. They affect our perspective of what's possible, shape how we interact with others and ourselves, and are often embedded in commonly accepted truths.

I've included a variety of examples to give you a broad understanding of how limiting beliefs show up. While I can't cover every possibility, the goal is to provide a strong starting point so you can recognize and challenge these blockers in your own life.

It can be frustrating to realize that the beliefs you accepted were actually holding you back. Instead of staying stuck, embrace this opportunity to step into a bigger, more empowered, more fulfilling, and truer-to-you chapter of your life.

Now, let's go think BIG.

TAUGHT TO BE SMALL

The crowd claps and sings along as Miley celebrates winning her first Grammy. She performs her song "Flowers," about loving herself better than her ex ever could—we all know who she's talking about.[1]

Moments like these feel empowering because when we watch someone overcome an obstacle, their victory feels like our own. On the surface, the challenge seems to be a bad romantic relationship. But the real struggle wasn't with someone else; it was Miley's relationship with herself, shaped by her thoughts and the way she was conditioned to think. (Not picking on Miley—this is something we all go through.)

We're taught to believe that happiness and self-worth depend on having a partner. This idea is reinforced by nearly every aspect of our environment—love songs with lyrics about not being able to live without someone, movies where finding "the one" is the ultimate happy ending, and commercials subtly suggesting that the perfect relationship equals a perfect life. With so much pressure, some people start defining their value by their relationship status, believing they're incomplete until someone comes along to love, care for, and finally "complete" them.

But there was never anything missing in the first place. As Miley realized—and as many people don't until much later in life—the person who will love you best is you. This doesn't mean relationships aren't valuable; it means they should add to our happiness, not be the source of it. You are your own greatest friend and cheerleader. And while it may sound cliché, it's true: when you build self-love, other love will follow.

So while the crowd cheers for Miley's empowerment, they also need to reflect on the deeper issue: like most of us, she was misled from the start.

WHAT ARE LIMITING BELIEFS?

Limiting beliefs are thoughts that hold you back from reaching your full potential. They convince you that you're not worthy, change isn't possible, happiness depends on external factors, and that you don't have value simply as you are.

These beliefs come from societal conditioning and build up over time. For example, if you're taught that failure is the opposite of success instead of proof that you tried, you develop a fear of it. This fear makes you see past experiences as setbacks rather than opportunities to grow. The more you avoid trying, the more stuck you feel, creating a cycle that convinces you you're not capable or that you don't belong.

Mental barriers shape how you see yourself and the world. They make challenges seem bigger, opportunities scarcer, and people more negative than they actually are. It's like thinking you're drowning when, in reality, the water is only two feet deep—all you have to do is stand up. And because these beliefs run in the background, you often don't realize their impact.

These beliefs fuel self-doubt, imposter syndrome, perfectionism, and self-sabotage. They influence relationships, society, and even human progress, making it harder to set boundaries, reinforcing harmful cultural norms, and dividing people based on race, gender, and other identities. In extreme cases, they can even be life-threatening. If someone believes vaccines cause autism, they might refuse medical care, putting themselves or their children at serious risk of preventable diseases.[2]

Limiting beliefs also create a domino effect that shapes every aspect of life. If you don't think you're capable of negotiating a higher salary, you'll likely settle for less, leading to financial stress and fewer opportunities. If you don't believe you're worthy of love, you might stay in a toxic relationship that affects your happiness and self-worth. Over time, these beliefs distort reality, making you feel like you have to earn your worth and prove your value just to be accepted.

They can even cause you to walk away from good opportunities or people simply because they don't fit the version of life you were conditioned to expect. And rigid beliefs take the joy out of life, making you feel like you need to be serious, have everything figured out, or follow a set path. But imagine how much lighter life would feel with more joy, more curiosity, and less pressure to be perfect all the time.

In this section, we'll talk more about how limiting beliefs shape our lives. But it's important to note that their true impact is immeasurable, reaching far beyond what can be listed or calculated.

WHERE LIMITATIONS COME FROM

Limiting beliefs are widespread—in cultural ideas, history, and even well-intentioned advice from family and friends. While this may seem overwhelming, it's actually an opportunity to build self-awareness, ask questions, and challenge the beliefs that shape our thinking.

These blockers likely formed in early human societies, where survival depended on caution and learned behaviors (e.g., "I can't venture too far, or I might be eaten by a predator"). While danger wasn't always present, generalizations were a necessary survival mechanism—aka better safe than sorry.

As societies evolved, religions and philosophies introduced belief systems that shaped what people could do or achieve. Some of these beliefs were beneficial, like encouraging social etiquette (say "please" and "thank you"). However, others became restrictive, limiting personal potential, creating division, and shaping negative perceptions of the world and others.

Here are some examples:

- **Caste System (Hinduism):** Restricted social mobility, reinforcing rigid divisions and limiting opportunities based on birth.
- **Fate and Destiny (Various Religions):** Encouraged the belief that life's path was predetermined, discouraging people from taking control of their circumstances.
- **Divine Right of Kings (Christianity, European Monarchies):** Maintained unquestioned authority by discouraging challenges to rulers and reinforcing rigid hierarchies.
- **Taboo and Ritual Purity (Various Religions):** Restricted social interactions, career opportunities, and access to resources for those deemed "unclean," reinforcing discrimination.
- **The Five Relationships (Confucian Philosophy):** Enforced strict social roles, discouraging mobility and limiting the pursuit of equality or justice.
- **The Sin of Forbidden Knowledge (Christianity, Medieval Thought):** Stifled intellectual exploration by labeling certain knowledge as dangerous or sinful, slowing scientific and philosophical progress.

- **The Afterlife as Ultimate Goal (Various Religions):** Shifted focus away from self-growth and present-day issues like social injustice, poverty, and suffering.

Limiting beliefs have been passed down for centuries by influential figures, becoming so ingrained that we rarely stop to question them.

Take René Descartes, for example. A 17th-century French philosopher, he made major contributions to mathematics, but some of his widely accepted ideas held us back for centuries (and still do). One of the most damaging was his claim that "animals don't have souls or consciousness."

Though later disproven—studies show even goldfish have memories and emotions—this belief has been used to justify cruelty, factory farming, and the dismissal of animal intelligence.[3] It has also contributed to a broader lack of empathy, leading many to exploit life for profit.

Then there's his mind-body dualism, the idea that the mind and body are separate. Also debunked, it still shapes modern thinking, fueling the neglect of mental health's impact on physical well-being and contributing to ongoing stigma and misinformation.

And, of course, his famous "I think, therefore I am" has led many to believe they *are* their thoughts. A more accurate way to put it would be, "I think, therefore I observe my thoughts." This small shift matters. We are the awareness behind our thoughts, not the thoughts themselves, and learning to manage them (like you're doing here) is key. Otherwise, they control us instead of the other way around.

While it may seem like I'm picking on Descartes, he's just one example. Sigmund Freud,[4] Charles Darwin,[5] Plato,[6] and countless others have left their marks, limiting how we understand ourselves and the world.[7] Their influence heightened by the limiting belief that we cannot and should not question established authority.

I often wonder if these thinkers imagined their ideas would be treated as absolute truths, causing unnecessary suffering long after being disproven. Would they take it back if they could? And if they did, would it even matter? Would anyone listen?

Take William James, for example. Part of his research on human consciousness was turned into the myth that "we only use ten percent of our brain." He attempted to correct this misconception, calling it "wholly misunderstood," but the myth stuck.[8] Decades later, people still believe it, and in 2014, the movie *Lucy* reignited the rumor.

But limiting beliefs aren't just relics of the past. They show up in everyday advice, often from people who assume their formula for success should be yours. There are rules about what you *should* do, *when* you should do it, and what's possible for you.

I see this a lot in writing. A popular book for writers advises, "never start a large writing project on any

Monday in December," as it claims you are "setting your-self up for failure."[9] But this is my fourth book, and I write on Mondays just fine. Another writer told me they heard the first 45 minutes of writing is a waste, so they wait before starting. I don't wait—I just write. If I waited, this book wouldn't be here.

And it's not just advice from books. It comes from well-meaning (or not-so-well-meaning) friends, family, and others:

- the aunt who limits your options by insisting that having kids is the only true path to fulfillment,
- the uncle who narrows your potential by telling you that a "real job" is the only way to succeed,
- the friend who creates a negative mindset around dating by saying, "all men are trash," and
- the investor who confidently declares that no one will ever read your book series because he "knows what people want." (Yes, this happened, and hey, thanks for proving him wrong.)

Many limiting beliefs are reinforced by common sayings like "That's just the way things are," or "Some people are just lucky." These seemingly harmless phrases subtly teach us to accept limitations that aren't real. Like:

- **"Emotions are weakness" / "Boys don't cry"** discourages emotional expression, leading people to suppress feelings until they surface in harmful ways like rage or self-harm.[10] It also makes them more vulnerable to emotional manipulation.

- **"Blood is thicker than water"** prioritizes family loyalty over personal well-being, making it difficult to set boundaries with toxic family members.
- **"You can't teach an old dog new tricks"** discourages growth and adaptability by implying people can't change as they age.
- **"Time heals all wounds"** suggests that time itself will heal pain, discouraging people from actively addressing their emotional or physical struggles.
- **"What doesn't kill you makes you stronger"** implies that suffering always leads to growth, which can justify enduring harmful situations.
- **"Everything happens for a reason"** suggests that every event has a purpose, preventing people from fully processing their experiences and taking responsibility for creating change in their lives.
- **"You have to pay your dues"** implies that success only comes after suffering, leading people to accept unnecessary hardship or exploitation.

Adding insult to injury, many of these concepts are often misunderstood. For example, "Blood is thicker than water" is actually a shortened version of "The blood of the covenant is thicker than the water of the womb," which originally meant that chosen bonds can be stronger than family ties. But over time, the shortened version has been used to justify tolerating toxic family dynamics, making people feel obligated to accept poor treatment just because they're related.

Misconceptions like this are common and shape our thinking in ways we don't realize. We might assume the loudest person is the strongest or mistake flashy possessions for wealth. But volume doesn't equal strength, and material things don't guarantee financial stability. In my experience, the wealthiest people aren't flashy, and those who appear rich are often drowning in debt or just one missed paycheck away from financial trouble.

TV and music reinforce limiting beliefs, and because beliefs are just thoughts we've repeated until they feel true, music's natural repetition makes us even more likely to internalize certain ideas. If a song keeps telling you, "You're nobody till somebody loves you,"[11] you might start to believe it. The same goes for TV, where stereotypes and narratives are repeated so often that they begin to feel like truth.

And the mecca of limiting beliefs is social media. Scroll through any app, and you'll find influencers stating their opinions as facts, followed by commenters fighting to push their own beliefs.

While some posts are insightful, many are just noise designed to provoke fear, outrage, or engagement through shock and outrage. A common one in my feed is men telling women how to dress, act, or exist in subservient roles. Even when I block the accounts or ignore them, they just keep coming. A dime a dozen.

BEYOND LIMITATIONS

No one is born believing they're not enough. Babies don't apologize for crying or feel guilty for needing love. But over time, society, culture, and experiences embed beliefs that whisper, "You're too much." "You're not enough." "You should be ashamed." These aren't truths; they're inherited stories passed down by those trapped in the same narratives.

While this might sound heavy, the great news is that we don't have to keep believing these blockers. When we challenge these ideas and rewrite the script, we reclaim our true selves—the part of us that was always worthy, always enough, and never broken. Instead of living from fear, we start living from possibility.

By removing our limitations, we lead by example, creating a ripple effect. The more we embrace our true selves, the more we give others permission to do the same. And in doing so, we don't just change our own lives; we help transform the world around us. We may even rediscover the dreams we abandoned as kids because someone told us they weren't possible. You know, you can literally buy an entire cake and eat it for breakfast if you want; you don't need to ask for permission. (Not that I recommend this. I'm just here to show you what you can do.)

Before we move on to identifying limiting beliefs in your mindset, I want to share a quote with you that resonated with me:

> *"If in this book harsh words are spoken about some of the greatest among the intellectual leaders of mankind, my motive is not, I hope, the wish to belittle them. It springs rather from my conviction that, if our civilization is to survive, we must break with the habit of deference to great men."* —Karl R. Popper, *The Open Society and Its Enemies*[12]

SPOTTING LIMITS

Before you can think big, you need to recognize when you're holding yourself back. The tricky part is that limiting beliefs often become so ingrained in your thinking that you don't question them.

Here are some common signs:

- **Fear-Driven:** Assuming the worst without proof. *If I ask for a raise, they'll think I'm greedy.*
- **Self-Doubt:** Focusing on flaws and past failures. *I messed up before, so I'll fail again.*
- **Paralyzing:** Procrastinating or avoiding. *It's just not the right time.*
- **Outdated:** Romanticizing the past or resisting change. *The good old days were better.*
- **Blame-Shifting:** Avoiding responsibility. *That's just the way the world works.*
- **Scarcity:** Believing success, money, or

opportunities are limited. *If they succeed, that means there's less for me.*

- **Identity-Based:** Tying limitations to characteristics like skin color, gender, or background. *Because of who I am, I can't succeed.*
- **Fixed:** Assuming abilities, circumstances, or challenges are set in stone. *That's just the way things are.*

On a personal level, staying small often shows up in how you think about yourself and your potential. These beliefs—some conscious, some not—shape what you believe you can achieve. Thoughts like *I'm not smart enough to try that* or *People like me don't succeed* keep you from trying, learning new things, or stepping outside your comfort zone.

But limiting beliefs aren't inherent; they're learned. You absorb them from your environment, culture, and upbringing. If you were told that success is only for a select few or that *"people like you"* shouldn't aim too high, you may have accepted those limits as truth. But here's the kicker: most of these ideas aren't based in reality. They're just stories that have been passed down, reinforced, and repeated until they feel real.

On a societal level, limiting beliefs can be just as damaging. For centuries, women were expected to stay home, while certain racial and social groups were denied access to education, jobs, and basic rights. These barriers limit everyone, including those who create or "benefit" from them, by creating a world with fewer ideas, perspectives, and chances to grow.[1]

It might sound shocking, but there's no scientific evidence to suggest that one skin color or gender is inherently better or worse than another. These are just made-up "rules" that someone created. And while men are often seen as stronger due to physical strength, science shows that women have greater endurance.[2] So who's "stronger" really depends on how you define strength.

Comparisons are just distractions rooted in the limiting belief that our worth depends on how we measure up to others. It's a waste of time and energy. And it's easy to say you should spend less time arguing with strangers online and more time with loved ones, but many people don't feel like they have loved ones to turn to—often because limiting beliefs about connection keep them isolated.

If you believe you're unworthy of deep relationships or that people will reject the real you, it's easy to pull away. But the need for connection doesn't go away, which is why so many people seek it in online debates, even when it leaves them feeling emptier.

What's even more tragic is that science shows most people actually support diversity,[3] and "being around people who are different from us makes us more creative, diligent, and hard-working."[4] So by holding on to these limiting beliefs, you ignore your true wants while limiting our potential to grow, collaborate, and build a better world for everyone.

Limiting beliefs are rigid, fear-driven, and negative. They make you jump to conclusions, like assuming you'll be rejected if you ask for a raise, believing you'll never find love, or hesitating to set boundaries because you're afraid of how others will react.

Self-doubt and a lack of boundaries often stem from the belief that you're not worthy of or don't deserve happiness and healthy relationships. It's easy to think, *Nah, that's not me.* But these beliefs often operate beneath the surface, shaping your choices in ways you don't realize. They show up in small habits like downplaying achievements, overcommitting, or refusing to ask for help when you need it.

That's why limiting beliefs are often called "blockers." They create mental roadblocks that keep you stuck. You tell yourself you'll look for a better job *tomorrow*, start a gym routine *when things calm down*, or put yourself out there *when you feel more confident*. And when nothing changes, it's easy to fall into the trap of thinking, *That's just how I am* or *This is just the way things are*, stopping growth before it even starts.

Blockers create a scarcity mindset and the belief that success, money, or opportunities are limited. This leads to the feeling that someone else's win takes something away from you, fueling resentment and low self-esteem. If a coworker gets a promotion, you might immediately compare yourself, questioning why you haven't advanced. To protect your ego, you may downplay their achievement or search for their "flaws" rather than seeing their success as proof that progress is possible.

Limiting beliefs can also lead to romanticizing the past, making you believe that things like this wouldn't have happened in the "good old days"—which is just another way to shield yourself from discomfort. They also keep you tied to outdated thinking, like staying loyal to a job that wouldn't hesitate to replace you, assuming college is the only path to success, or believing that people can't truly change. (Spoiler alert: They can.)[5]

After reading about limiting beliefs, was anything surprising to you? Did any beliefs or thoughts you've heard in the past come to mind? How might they be holding you back? Take a moment to reflect on where these beliefs might be limiting your potential and keeping you stuck.

_____

_____

_____

_____

_____

Now, let's take a closer look at how these blockers might be showing up in your life.

IDENTIFYING BLOCKERS IN YOUR MINDSET

To uncover limiting beliefs in your mindset, review the statements below. Be honest with yourself and check all that apply.

With money and abundance, do you...
❏ believe there aren't enough resources, and others' success means less for you
❏ think opportunities are limited, and once missed, they'll never return
❏ feel that wanting more is greedy or unrealistic, so you should settle?
❏ believe you've missed your chance for the success you want
❏ think money is hard to come by, or that you must work nonstop to succeed financially
❏ assume wealthy people are just luckier or born into privilege
❏ feel guilty spending money on yourself or wanting more for yourself
____ checked

In social and romantic relationships, do you...
❏ believe people are inherently bad and cannot be trusted
❏ think true friends should always be there for everything, no matter the situation
❏ feel that you need to hide your true self to be accepted

❏ believe that a happy relationship means no conflict at all
❏ think your partner is meant to "complete" you and that you need a relationship to be happy
❏ assume love should be like the movies, with grand gestures and constant excitement
❏ feel obligated to tolerate bad behavior because of the length or type of relationship
___ checked

For career and growth do you...
❏ assume success requires following a traditional path, order, or timeline
❏ feel like you don't have or can't build the skills or experience to succeed
❏ avoid healthy risks because you fear mistakes will permanently damage your reputation
❏ believe that your job defines your worth and success
❏ avoid taking on new challenges due to fear of failure or the belief that you can't succeed
❏ feel stuck in your current situation and believe opportunities are out of reach
❏ think you have to be entirely self-made and that asking for help, mentorship, or networking is a sign of weakness
___ checked

In your worldview do you...
❏ believe the world is getting worse and nothing will ever improve

❏ think in terms of "us vs. them," seeing the world as full of dangers and threats

❏ feel powerless to make a difference

❏ assume TV, social media, and movies reflect reality

❏ often feel that life is unfair and bad things happen to good people

❏ believe that material possessions define a person's worth

❏ see the world as a place where bad things are inevitable and improvement is unlikely

___ checked

When it comes to self-view do you...

❏ think you can't achieve your dreams and feel inadequate when comparing yourself to others

❏ assume your past mistakes define who you are and that you're "damaged"

❏ feel like you need approval from others to feel good about yourself

❏ believe you can't change certain things about yourself

❏ think everyone else has a perfect, healthy life and relationships, except for you

❏ rely on zodiac signs, lucky numbers, or time-lines to determine what's possible for you

❏ think you can't do something or go after what you want because of your gender, race, or age

___ checked

SCORING AND REFLECTION

Did any blockers stand out to you? Review the sections where you checked the most items. Do you notice any patterns? Do these thoughts arise regularly, or only when you're rushed or stressed? How long have you been holding onto these beliefs, and how might they be shaping your actions or decisions?

_____

_____

_____

_____

_____

HOW LIMITING BELIEFS SHAPE YOUR LIFE

Just one limiting belief can cause ripple effects that disrupt your overall well-being. When you think you need to hide your true self to be accepted, you're telling yourself you're not worthy as you are. This can lead to self-abandonment, chasing approval, and staying in relationships that don't truly fulfill you. If you believe relationships are the key to happiness, you may become an easy target for manipulative people who take from you while you give. These people-pleasing behaviors, driven by the need for validation, make it harder to set boundaries and prioritize your own needs.

Believing a friend should always be there for you no matter what can strain relationships. While friendships are important, expecting unwavering availability ignores life's realities—family, responsibilities, and personal growth must take priority at times. Healthy relationships allow space for each person to balance their commitments without guilt.

If you think you can't achieve your dreams, you may feel stuck and unmotivated. Comparing yourself to others only deepens feelings of inadequacy, making you feel behind in both personal and professional life. Letting past mistakes define you creates a cycle of self-judgment, preventing growth and keeping you from learning from those experiences. And even when you're given an opportunity you've earned, you may struggle to appreciate it, feeling like you don't truly deserve it. This sense of not being good enough —often called impostor syndrome—can keep you from fully embracing your success, making you doubt yourself instead of recognizing your own hard work and abilities. But the truth is, you're more capable than you think.

Seeking constant approval from others makes it difficult to trust your own abilities and decisions and stops you from building confidence. This leads to trouble accepting compliments or praise, often because of a lack of self-acceptance or fear of appearing arrogant. When you prioritize external validation, you allow other people's thoughts to dictate your self-worth, leaving you feeling uncertain and disconnected from your true wants and needs.

When you believe that certain things about yourself can't change, it limits your potential for growth. And thinking that everyone else has a perfect, healthy life or relationship can isolate you, making you feel like you're the only one struggling while everyone else has it all figured out. Similarly, using zodiac signs or lucky numbers as a lighthearted guide can be fun (I personally love them!), but relying on them to define your future can become restrictive, preventing you from taking responsibility for your own path.

If you assume life is inherently hard, you may focus on struggle and self-sabotage instead of looking for ways to make things easier. Believing the world is getting worse and that nothing will improve leads to hopelessness, making it hard to take action or see opportunities for change.

Thinking that most people are selfish and only act in their own interests fuels distrust and weakens your ability to form meaningful connections. And feeling powerless to make a difference reinforces inaction, keeping you stuck in the belief that life is beyond your control.

Often, these limiting beliefs show up as a quiet voice in the back of your mind, questioning whether you're capable or worthy. You might doubt if you're good enough, if you deserve success, or if you have what it takes to change your circumstances. These thoughts can feel so natural that you don't even question them—but they're not facts. They're learned patterns that, over time, have shaped how you see yourself and the world. The good news is that once you recognize them, you can challenge and replace them.

POWER IN NEW PERSPECTIVES

Recognizing limiting beliefs can feel heavy or even discouraging. Right now, you're seeing them all at once in a condensed way, which can make them seem overwhelming. In daily life, though, you'll work through them one at a time, and it won't feel as intense.

At first, it might be frustrating to realize how these beliefs have shaped your choices or disheartening to think about the opportunities you may have missed. You may even feel resistant to questioning them, wondering if they really have that much control over you. But while this process can be uncomfortable, it's also freeing.

The more you bring these beliefs into the light, the easier they are to challenge. With time and effort, they'll lose their hold, and you'll gain a clearer, more confident perspective on yourself and your potential—along with the freedom, opportunities, and growth that come with it.

Now, let's talk about how to start changing them.

BREAKING THE BOX

Recognizing a limiting belief is one thing—changing it is another. You might realize that thoughts like *I'm not good enough* are holding you back, but that doesn't mean they disappear overnight. If it were that easy, we'd all walk around with limitless confidence and zero self-doubt.

So, how do you replace these blockers with something better? Start by understanding what it means to think big:

- **Evidence-Based:** Making decisions based on facts and possibilities instead of fear or assumptions. *I bring value to my job, so it's okay to ask for fair pay.*
- **Self-Belief:** Trusting that you can learn, improve, and handle challenges. *I'm not perfect, but I can improve with effort.*
- **Actionable:** Taking steps forward instead of

staying stuck in doubt. *I don't have to wait for the perfect moment. I can start now.*

- **Forward-thinking:** Looking ahead instead of staying stuck in the past. *I can learn from my mistakes and create new opportunities.*
- **Ownership:** Taking responsibility for what you can control instead of blaming circumstances. *My choices shape my future.*
- **Abundance:** Believing there are plenty of opportunities for success. *Someone else's win doesn't take away from mine.*
- **Merit-based:** Believing your potential is not limited by or tied to your gender, race, or background. *My abilities and success are shaped by my actions and mindset.*
- **Growth:** Knowing you can get better at things with practice and effort. *With time and learning, I can improve and reach my goals.*

Your beliefs shape what you focus on. With an empowered mindset, you see the world as full of opportunities rather than obstacles. Challenges are inevitable, but so is progress, and every step forward contributes to positive change. Instead of assuming people are selfish, you recognize that most are doing their best—and that meaningful connections can lead to growth.

When you believe problems are solvable, you approach challenges with creativity and optimism. The world no longer feels like a constant threat, but rather a place of both beauty and difficulties. You also become more discerning about media portrayals, choosing to focus on stories of kindness, innovation, and progress. Understanding that life isn't always fair, you shift from a defeated mentality to one of empowerment, knowing growth and positive change are always possible.

With a growth mindset, you start believing your dreams are achievable, no matter your starting point. Mistakes become lessons rather than proof of failure. You trust your judgment, make decisions with confidence, and stop seeking constant approval from others. Accepting compliments and recognizing your worth becomes easier because you understand that growth is ongoing.

You also stop comparing yourself to an illusion of ideals. You understand that no one's life is perfect and everyone faces struggles. This awareness allows you to approach both yourself and others with self-compassion.

Adopting empowering beliefs shifts your approach to life. You make decisions based on logic and possibility, not fear. In your career, you advocate for fair pay or pursue new opportunities, knowing you bring value. If you're considered for a promotion, you trust that it's for a reason —you've earned it. With money, you see wealth as abundant and explore smarter ways to build it, like investing or leveraging your time, rather than competing with others.

Self-belief grows as you view challenges as learning opportunities. In relationships, you trust that with time and effort, you can form deep, meaningful connections.

At work, you accept that mistakes are part of the process, each one bringing you closer to success.

Taking action becomes key. Instead of waiting for the "right" moment, you take small steps toward your goals, whether it's learning a new skill, applying for a job, or simply planting the seed that new possibilities exist. And you take ownership of your choices. Whether in finances, career, or personal growth, you focus on what you *can* control instead of blaming circumstances.

An abundance mindset lets you see that there's room for everyone to succeed. In relationships, you celebrate other people's wins, knowing they don't diminish your own. In work and money, you choose collaboration over competition and recognize opportunities everywhere.

And when you don't tie your success to a specific identity or trait like gender, you free yourself from unnecessary limitations. Instead of being weighed down by people who try to define your potential based on race or gender, you recognize that their beliefs reflect their own conditioning—not reality. Rather than internalizing their limitations, you start questioning why they're so invested in making others believe in scarcity and restriction in the first place.

Most importantly, you trust in your ability to grow. You believe your skills and circumstances are flexible, and that each step forward builds momentum toward the life you want.

Now, think about times when you've thought big. When have you stepped out of your comfort zone, trusted your abilities, or embraced opportunities despite uncertainty? Maybe you took on a challenging project, spoke up for yourself, or made a decision that pushed you forward.

_____

_____

_____

_____

_____

Whatever the example, recognizing where you've overcome limiting beliefs shows that you already have the tools to navigate challenges with more confidence. The more you identify these moments, the easier it will be to challenge and shift blockers moving forward.

RETHINKING YOUR BELIEFS

The next step in overcoming limiting beliefs is to challenge them. This doesn't mean fighting or suppressing your thoughts, but questioning them and deciding if they truly reflect reality. A belief might _feel_ true, but that doesn't mean it is.

The best way to figure this out is by asking where the belief came from, looking for counterexamples, reframing your thoughts, and seeing how much it's really affecting your life. But before you get into that, it helps to be in the right mindset.

Most of us are harder on ourselves than we are on others, which makes it tough to recognize when we're holding ourselves back. To challenge limiting beliefs effectively, you need to separate who you are from what you think and take a fair, objective view. A simple way to do this is by asking: *Would I say this to a friend?*

We tend to be much kinder and more reasonable when giving advice to others. If a friend told you they weren't "good enough" to apply for a job or try something new, you'd probably remind them of all the reasons they are. Applying that same perspective to yourself will help you step back and see your thoughts more clearly. (Journaling can also help.)

To stay objective, here are four things to keep in mind:

1. **No one is more or less deserving than anyone else.** Whether you're a CEO, a cashier, a celebrity, or a student, everyone deserves respect. Remembering this can help break down limiting beliefs about status, worth, and potential.

2. **Everyone has the ability to grow and change.** Your brain is literally wired for growth and neuroplasticity shows we can build new habits and improve at any age. So the idea that you're "stuck" or "too old to change" simply isn't true.

3. **You have the power to choose.** You can't control everything, but you *can* control how you

respond. Your reactions shape your experiences, and remembering this helps break the feeling of powerlessness.

4. **Love and connection are fundamental human needs.** We all need meaningful relationships. When you focus on connection instead of fear, it helps break down limiting beliefs that make you feel isolated or unworthy.

Now, let's break down exactly how to challenge your limiting beliefs.

QUESTION AND SOURCE IT

Limiting beliefs often feel like hard truths, but they're usually just opinions, not facts. If you think you're too old, too young, or not skilled enough to succeed, ask yourself: *What proof do I have?* People of all ages and experience levels achieve success every day.

Many limiting beliefs come from family, culture, or media. If you believe "money is hard to come by" or "success isn't for people like me," ask: *Where did I learn that? Did I hear it growing up? Did I absorb it from social media?* Recognizing the source helps you be more objective and separate what's truly yours from what you've been taught.

Reflection Questions:

- Is this really true?
- Is this fact or just an opinion?

- Where did this belief come from, and who taught me this?

FLIP IT AND REVERSE IT –MISSY ELLIOTT

You can challenge limiting beliefs by flipping them and finding exceptions. If you think, *It's not the right time to start,* flip it to, *There will never be a perfect time, but I can start now.* Waiting for the "right moment" usually just leads to inaction.

And if you've been told that people who have been abused are doomed to repeat the cycle, flip it to, *Millions of survivors break the cycle and create healthy lives.* Looking for real-life examples that prove the opposite of your belief helps weaken its hold.

Reflection Questions:

- Where can I find proof this belief doesn't work?
- Where have I seen this belief not be true?
- What if the opposite were true?

CHECK YOUR WORDS AND BORROW CONFIDENCE

Remember the saying "Sticks and stones may break my bones, but words will never hurt me?" Yeah, that's a limiting belief, because words *do* shape reality. Pay attention to phrases like "I can't" or "I'm not." They often signal limiting beliefs that need reframing. Ask yourself: *How would someone without this belief act?*

For example, instead of saying, "I can't afford that," try reframing it as, "What if I could?" This won't instantly change your finances, but it shifts your mindset from limitation to possibility. And if you struggle with thinking *I'm not worthy of success*, imagine how someone without that belief would carry themselves. Borrow their confidence and act as though you already have greater self-worth, and your actions will start to reflect it.

Reflection Questions:

- How would someone without this belief act?
- What's one step I can take to act as though this belief isn't true?

LOOK AT THE RESULTS

If a belief keeps you stuck or unhappy, it's probably limiting or outdated. The best way to test it is to look at the results. Does thinking this way push you forward or hold you back? Does it bring peace or stress?

For example, if you think *I'll never be good with money,* you might avoid learning about finances, leading to ongoing financial struggles. If you believe *I'm not lovable,* you might settle for unhealthy relationships or push people away. These beliefs don't reflect reality; they reflect a self-fulfilling cycle.

Ask yourself: *What is this belief actually doing for me? Is it protecting me, or is it keeping me in the same cycle?* A belief that consistently leads to negative outcomes isn't true; it's just a script you've been following. Rewrite it.

Reflection Questions:

- How has this belief impacted my decisions and opportunities?
- Does this belief bring me closer to or further from the life I want?
- If I challenge this belief, what might change?

Think about the blocker(s) you identified earlier. What if the belief wasn't true? How would your choices, actions, or opportunities change? Challenge yourself to find at least one example—whether from your life, the life of someone you know, or even a public figure—where this belief doesn't hold up. What does that tell you?

_____

_____

_____

_____

_____

WHO PROFITS FROM SMALL THINKING?

Another way to challenge limiting beliefs is to ask who benefits from them. Plenty of industries and influencers profit when you doubt yourself, feel stuck, or believe you're not enough. When you feel powerless, someone else gets to sell you the solution.

And since people strongly identify with their beliefs, those pushing these ideas need you to adopt their way of thinking in order to gain. Whether it's an industry, a person, or a system, they rely on your belief in their narrative to maintain control, continue profiting, and stay relevant.

Recognizing who benefits will help you challenge limiting beliefs. Here are a few examples:

> **The Cosmetic Industry** makes billions by convincing you that you need constant improvement. There's nothing wrong with enjoying makeup or skincare, but when it's marketed as a necessity to be "enough," it becomes a problem. Confidence doesn't drive sales, but insecurity does.

> **The Pharmaceutical Industry** profits when you see mental health as only a chemical imbalance that can only be fixed with medication.[1] While medication has its place, relying on it without exploring therapy, lifestyle changes, or deeper healing keeps you dependent—and that keeps the money flowing.

> **Podcasters and Influencers** thrive by making you feel like the world is hopeless, success is impossi-

ble, or the system is rigged against you. The more powerless or outraged you feel, the more you stay engaged, driving up their views, shares, and ad revenue.

Politicians benefit when you have a limited view of the world and policies, making it easier for them to push fear-based narratives, expand their power, and keep people divided instead of questioning the system.

Education Systems That Discourage Critical Thinking rely on you following rules instead of questioning them. When you aren't taught to challenge ideas, you're more likely to accept things as they are rather than push for change. That keeps power in the hands of institutions.

Diet Culture and Fitness Fads make money by convincing you that you're never quite there. Never thin enough, strong enough, or disciplined enough. There's always another plan, supplement, or program to buy, and the goalposts keep moving to ensure the cycle continues.

People With Limiting Beliefs reinforce them to justify their own choices. It's not always intentional, and sometimes, they just don't want to feel alone in their thinking. Misery loves company, and when you're surrounded by people stuck in small thinking, it's easy to stay the same.

While these industries profit from the limiting belief that you need something external to succeed, an even bigger limiting belief is that you need these industries and influencers in the first place. The truth is, they need you.

Companies can't profit without consumers, and for podcasters and influencers, the risk of you rejecting their beliefs is even greater. Since they tie their identity to these beliefs, if you don't subscribe to what they're saying, it can feel like a threat to their sense of worth. This often leads them to double down, reinforcing their narrative even harder to keep you on board.

When you stop engaging with their narratives and question what's being sold to you, you weaken their influence. It might seem like not listening won't make a difference, but research shows that just 3.5% of a population is enough to create meaningful change.[2]

By recognizing who benefits from making you feel "less than" or from selling beliefs that boost your ego by putting others down, you start challenging those narratives and thinking bigger in your daily life. And the more you challenge these ideas, the less control they have over you.

Who profits from your insecurity and dependence? How can you tap into your own ability to thrive independently and shift the power away from them?

_____

_____

_____

Thinking big allows you to make decisions based on facts, values, and long-term goals rather than being driven by doubt or fleeting emotions. When you catch yourself thinking, *I can't do this,* stop and ask, *why not?* Why can't you succeed in a new position? You've overcome challenges before. Why can't you push past self-doubt? Every time you reframe a limiting belief, you open the door to new perspectives and possibilities.

Challenging limiting beliefs also means not identifying with your beliefs and keeping them flexible. It's about staying open to growth rather than tying your identity to any single viewpoint. It's recognizing that no one has all the answers, and we're all still learning. Just look at how much has been discovered about the human body, psychology, and the universe in the past few decades.

Not long ago, experts believed the adult brain couldn't change. Now, we know thoughts and behaviors can rewire it. Many people assume everything has already been figured out, but new discoveries about cells, proteins, and the human body are made almost every day.

You often hear bold claims presented as facts, and they spread quickly. But when they turn out to be false, the correction rarely gets the same attention. Take the claim that people quickly become abusive when given power. The Stanford Prison Experiment, a 1971 study, seemed to prove this idea. It suggested that ordinary people, when placed in positions of authority, would become cruel and oppressive. The study became one of psychology's most famous examples of human nature's dark side, cited in textbooks, documentaries, and even legal cases.

But later investigations revealed serious flaws. The participants were coached to act in extreme ways, and the results weren't as spontaneous as originally claimed. When researchers tried to replicate the experiment, they didn't get the same outcome. One key finding was that participants' aggression stemmed not from the corrupting influence of power, but from their desire to please the researchers.[3] This challenges the widely held belief that power alone makes people cruel, suggesting instead that the need for approval played a bigger role. Yet, despite these issues, the original study's message— that power corrupts quickly—had already cemented itself as common knowledge.

This doesn't mean people are out to deceive you or that you're constantly being misled. It's a mix of sensationalized information getting attention and a lack of understanding about having a growth mindset. As a result, people get stuck in their beliefs and resist change, even when presented with new information.

You need to take responsibility for questioning what you hear, looking for facts, and staying open to new perspectives. Balance is key. There's a lot to learn from others, but it's just as important to think for yourself and consider intentions. The goal isn't to doubt everything, but to stay curious and thoughtful.

You don't need to have all the answers, just a willingness to rethink beliefs that no longer serve you and consider new information. Changing the way you think takes time, and it won't always feel natural at first. But remember, emotion follows thought. The more you practice new ways of thinking, the more confident you'll feel, creating a positive cycle that helps you break old patterns and move forward.

Now, let's talk about how to make these changes stick.

VIEW FROM THE TOP

Sometimes, changing a limiting belief is simple. You hear a new perspective, and suddenly, the old belief doesn't make sense anymore. Maybe you thought, *I'll never be good at networking,* but then someone shares a tip that makes it easier, and just like that, your belief shifts.

But deep-seated beliefs, the ones that have shaped your self-image for years, don't always budge so easily. If the thought *I'm not enough* has been ingrained in you for a long time, a single reframe to *I am enough* won't make it disappear overnight. Doubt creeps back in. Old thought patterns resurface. This is where many people get stuck, and that's why evaluation is so important.

When a belief doesn't change easily, you need something stronger than just a new thought. You need motivation to keep pushing forward. Evaluating the benefits of reframing a limiting belief gives you that motivation so you'll keep going, even when it feels tough.

When we evaluate, we:

- Identify the actions that will move us forward
- See how reducing limiting beliefs brings us closer to our goals (and how freeing that feels)
- Recognize the obstacles that make change difficult so we can work through them instead of giving up

Let's break it down.

ACTIONS YOU CAN TAKE TO IMPROVE YOUR SITUATION

Changing your mindset doesn't happen overnight, and you don't have to take huge leaps to make progress. Small, consistent steps lead to real change. If you believe *I'm not athletic*, start with a ten-minute walk instead of diving into an intense workout. Small wins build momentum and make bigger changes feel more natural over time.

Your environment also plays a big role in shaping your beliefs. If you're surrounded by negativity or doubt, it's harder to break free from limiting thoughts. Seek out communities, books, and mentors that reinforce growth and possibility. Surrounding yourself with positive influences makes it easier to adopt empowering beliefs.

Here are a few ways to take action right now:

- **Test Your Beliefs:** Instead of assuming something is true, put it to the test. If you think, *I'll never be good at public speaking,* sign up for a small speaking opportunity or practice in front of a friend. Gather real-world evidence that challenges your belief.
- **Challenge Limiting Assumptions:** If you think, *I can't apply for a job unless I meet every single requirement,* apply anyway. Even if you don't get the job, you'll prove to yourself that you can. (Fun fact: many employers prioritize potential over a perfect resume.)
- **Take Steps Toward Connection:** If you believe, *I can't have a healthy relationship because I've been hurt before,* open yourself up to new connections. Even if things don't go perfectly, each step forward reinforces the truth that your past doesn't dictate your future.

Sometimes, just thinking about a new idea can help you move forward, but real change happens when you take action. That's what makes the difference between progress and wishful thinking. You don't have to feel completely ready. Just start, or you'll wish you had. The more you act on your new beliefs, the stronger they become.

HOW REDUCING LIMITING BELIEFS HELPS YOU REACH YOUR GOALS (AND HOW GOOD THAT WILL FEEL)

Imagine waking up tomorrow without the limiting beliefs that hold you back. No hesitation before speaking up in meetings. No fear of failure stopping you from taking risks. No voice in your head saying you can't.

Reducing limiting beliefs isn't just about achieving more, it's about experiencing life differently. Here's just some of what happens when you start thinking big:

1. **You Become More Confident:** When you stop believing *I'm not smart enough* or *I don't belong here*, you start showing up differently. You take up space, speak with conviction, and trust your own decisions.

2. **You Find More Opportunities:** Limiting beliefs keep you stuck in hesitation. Without them, you're more likely to say yes to that job, that relationship, or that new challenge because you no longer assume failure.

3. **You Feel More In Control:** Instead of feeling like life is happening *to* you, you realize you have a say in how things unfold. You stop defaulting to self-doubt and start choosing action over fear.

4. **You Enjoy Life More:** Without the weight of constant self-criticism, you can actually appreciate your accomplishments, relationships,

and experiences. You stop waiting for the other shoe to drop and start allowing happiness in.

5. **You Reach Your Goals Faster:** When you believe you're capable, you waste less time second-guessing yourself and more time executing. Progress comes easier because you're no longer sabotaging yourself.

The best part is that these changes don't just affect one area of your life. When you remove limitations, everything shifts: your career, relationships, and overall happiness. It's not just about success. It's about finally feeling free.

THE OBSTACLES THAT ARE PREVENTING CHANGE: IT'S NOT JUST "FIND AND REPLACE"

If changing limiting beliefs were as simple as just swapping them out, we'd all be walking around with unshakable confidence and perfect mindsets. But it's not that easy. Sometimes, there are deeper forces at play, internal processes that make it hard to remove blockers, even when they hold you back. And sometimes, challenging beliefs—whether our own or society's—triggers resistance.

Harvard economist Roland Fryer Jr. experienced this first hand after he took a data-driven look at police brutality. After analyzing millions of data points from police departments, he found something unexpected:

While police used force more often on some racial groups, there wasn't clear proof of bias in police shootings.[1]

Instead of sparking discussion, his research sparked outrage. Many people were furious. Not because his methods were flawed, but because his findings contradicted what they deeply believed to be true. The backlash was so severe that Fryer had to hire security.

While unsettling, his experience is a perfect example of how hard it can be to accept information that challenges our beliefs, even when it's backed by facts. This outward reaction reflects the inner struggle you may face when trying to challenge your own limiting beliefs.

Our brains don't like change, and they definitely don't like being wrong. Even when a belief is limiting, you may cling to it because it feels familiar and safe. Here are a few of the mental roadblocks that make reframing beliefs so difficult:

- **Self-Fulfilling Prophecy:** If you believe something strongly enough, you unconsciously make it come true. So if you think you're terrible at relationships, you might sabotage good ones just to prove yourself right.
- **Learned Helplessness:** Repeated failures can make you believe trying is pointless, even when circumstances change. Like an elephant tied to a small rope that once held it back, you stop trying even when you could break free.

- **Cognitive Dissonance & Self-Justification:**
  When new information contradicts your beliefs,
  your brain resists. Instead of changing your
  views, you justify them to avoid discomfort,
  convincing yourself that you were always right.
- **Familiarity Bias:** Even flawed beliefs feel "safe"
  if they're all we've ever known. The unknown is
  scary, so you stick with what's comfortable, even
  when it holds you back.
- **Belief-Based Identity & Ego-Investment:** When
  beliefs become part of who you are, questioning
  them can feel like questioning yourself. If you tie
  your self-worth to being "right," admitting you
  were wrong feels like failure so you defend your
  beliefs at all costs.

Another obstacle to challenging limiting beliefs is the
"comfort zone." This term has become a bit of a buzz-
word in recent years and can feel like jargon, but there's
truth to it. The comfort zone isn't always about feeling
comfortable in the way you expect. It's often a place filled
with frustration, sadness, and self-doubt. But because it's
familiar, you stay there. You hold onto limiting beliefs
like, *I don't deserve good things* or *The world is a dangerous
place,* because it feels safer than facing the unknown.

What's even more challenging is that for many of us,
happiness can feel like something too unfamiliar, too
scary. We're used to playing small, staying within the
confines of our self-doubt and frustration. So, the idea of
being truly happy feels out of reach. In fact, many people

fear that happiness might be temporary—that it will be snatched away by some dramatic event, much like the plot of many movies.

But here's the truth: overcoming limiting beliefs is often less about acquiring more success or proving something and more about allowing happiness in. It's about learning how to be happy and rejecting the narrative that happiness can't last, that it's too fragile to hold onto. In many ways, removing blockers is about giving ourselves permission to be happy and embracing the fact that you *deserve* it.

Hearing about blockers and the obstacles that can keep you stuck may feel heavy, but simply knowing about them reduces their power. And with confidence, you can weaken them even more.

Confidence doesn't mean you won't experience setbacks. It means you'll keep going despite them. Repeated failures may still make you feel like trying is pointless, but you'll bounce back and eventually try again. And while admitting you're wrong may still feel uncomfortable, confidence helps you separate your identity from your beliefs. Instead of seeing mistakes as proof of failure, you will recognize them as opportunities to grow.

Building this kind of self-awareness takes practice, and one of the best ways to strengthen it is by consistently reframing your thoughts.

JUST KEEP SWIMMING – SMALL STEPS, BIG CHANGES

To help you continue this practice, I want to introduce a simple yet powerful framework called the ICE Method. I created this method to help cool "hot thoughts" (aka, the ones that loop in our minds and hold us back), and you can also use it to break through blockers to expand your thinking.

The ICE Method:

1. Identify limiting beliefs
2. Challenge and change those beliefs so they no longer limit you
3. Evaluate how thinking big will improve your life

When you were spotting limits, you were identifying. Breaking the box was about challenging those beliefs, and here, you've been evaluating what life looks like when you move beyond them. So don't tell yourself you can't do this; you already have.

You have the tools to get started, but it's up to you to keep challenging your limiting beliefs. The more you reframe your thoughts, the easier it becomes. Reflecting on your thinking, like we've done here, speeds up that process. Over time, you'll recognize limiting thoughts in real time and correct them as they happen. The more you do this, the more quickly you'll be able to catch yourself in the moment and make clearer, more intentional decisions.

I've included templates in the back of the book to help you apply this process. Here are some quick reminders to help you spot and reject limiting beliefs:

- What people say is what they think (unless proven fact)
- Common beliefs aren't always true
- If it limits you, question it
- *Can't* is usually *won't*
- Fear isn't proof
- One exception can break the rule
- Assumptions aren't reality
- Your past doesn't define your future
- Would you tell a friend to believe this?

Keep these in mind and remember: you don't have to go from *I'm not good enough* to *I'm the greatest*. But at the very least, recognize that you're capable and worthy. Changing old beliefs can feel overwhelming, but progress isn't about speed; it's about steady, consistent effort.

Now, let's look at some "rules" to help you continue thinking big.

5 RULES OF BIG THINK

RULE #1: I AM MY OWN GREATEST ADVOCATE

Have you ever needed help but stayed quiet, thinking you should handle everything on your own? Maybe you wondered where you stood in a relationship but were nervous to ask, "What are we?" Or wanted to ask for something, like a raise, but told yourself you should just be grateful for what you have?

Unfortunately, most of us were never taught to advocate for ourselves. Instead, we're taught to be agreeable, not ask for too much, and wait for recognition rather than demand it. Add limiting beliefs like "I don't deserve more" or "I don't want to be a burden" to the mix, and speaking up can feel nearly impossible. But when you understand what's reasonable and gain the confidence to stand up for yourself, everything shifts. You stop settling and start seeing possibilities and opportunities you hadn't considered before.

Self-advocacy isn't about being demanding or entitled. It's about recognizing your worth, communicating your needs, and pushing past the barriers that keep you silent. It's thinking big.

UNDERSTANDING AND ADVOCATING FOR YOUR NEEDS

The more you understand your needs, the better you can advocate for them. Needs are shaped by your individual values and circumstances, but there are some universal ones that we all share:

- **Safety:** Physical and emotional security, free from harm
- **Respect:** Being treated with dignity, heard, and valued
- **Autonomy:** Control over our own life and decisions
- **Meaningful Connections:** Building relationships and belonging
- **Basic Resources:** Access to essentials like food, shelter, and financial stability

Basic needs come up in everyday life more than you realize. Safety might mean feeling comfortable enough to speak up without worrying about backlash. Respect is knowing you deserve to be treated fairly at work, in relationships, and everywhere else. Autonomy is having control over your life and decisions instead of just going along with what's expected. And connections thrive when you communicate honestly instead of avoiding tough conversations.

You don't have to do everything alone (the idea of being self made is a limiting belief, we all need others to succeed), and it's completely reasonable to ask for help. While you may not want to define a relationship after a date or two, it's understandable to ask where things are going after a few weeks—especially if the other person doesn't want you to date other people or is making comments like, "Where have you been all my life?"

If you are underpaid or have taken on more responsibilities at work, asking for a raise doesn't make you ungrateful. It means you *are* grateful. You appreciate what you have and want your company to appreciate what they have in you, too. It's common corporate knowledge that employees who feel appreciated are more productive, so you're actually doing *them* a favor.

Learning to ask for your needs doesn't mean they will be met. Not everyone will help you when you ask, some people are confused and do not want to define relationships even when they don't want you dating other people, and not all companies will appreciate their employees. But don't let that stop you. There are people who will step up and help you, and there are people who want to have clarity in relationships, and companies who will appreciate their employees.

Focusing on what's reasonable and recognizing that your needs are common (and when they're fulfilled, lead to better outcomes for everyone) makes it easier for you to advocate for yourself with confidence. And if you've ever held back from asking for help, clarity, or fairness, you're not alone. You don't need to start asking for things tomorrow, simply planting the seed is enough to get the muscles moving.

UNDERSTANDING YOUR RIGHTS

You can't advocate for yourself if you don't know what protections exist. You have rights that protect you in everyday life. Here are a few:

- **Politics and Government:** Voting rights, free speech, and protections against discrimination in political participation.
- **Tenant:** Protections against unfair eviction, unsafe housing, and discrimination.
- **Consumer:** Safeguards against fraud, false advertising, and defective products.
- **Disability:** Laws ensuring equal access, reasonable accommodations, and protection from discrimination.
- **Family and Parental:** Custody rights, parental leave, child welfare protections, and family support services.
- **Criminal Justice:** Protections during interactions with law enforcement, fair trial rights, and safeguards against unlawful searches or arrests.
- **Privacy and Data:** Laws governing personal data, online privacy, and protections against surveillance or identity theft.

The foundation of self-advocacy is knowing what you're entitled to. At work or school, understand company policies, educational rights, and how to request accommodations or ask for help. In healthcare, know that you can ask questions, seek second opinions, and make informed decisions about your treatment. (I've personally avoided being prescribed unnecessary prescriptions, getting an unnecessary root canal, and an unnecessary ultrasound by getting second opinions.)

Change starts with action. If your rights are being ignored, do something: document issues, speak with HR, talk to counselors, or seek legal advice. If you're dealing with housing issues, research local tenant laws and connect with tenant unions or legal aid. Stay informed about politics, seek unbiased news, and stay engaged in elections. Contact your representatives—they're elected to serve you. Most importantly, vote.

Unfortunately, those who are supposed to advocate for you don't always follow through. As a child, you may not have had the support you needed from parents, teachers, or mentors, leaving your needs unmet or making you feel wrong, entitled, or needy for simply wanting reasonable things.

This doesn't mean *you* were wrong. It likely means *they* couldn't meet your needs or were never taught to advocate for themselves, so they saw your reasonable requests as a threat. For example, if someone grew up believing that speaking up is disrespectful, they might view your self-advocacy as overstepping rather than a basic right.

While this doesn't excuse their behavior, it helps explain it.

As an adult, the pattern can continue—a manager ignoring workplace concerns, a school failing to provide support, or politicians prioritizing donors over voters.

When the advocacy you need doesn't happen, it can shape how you see your worth and ability to stand up for yourself. If self-advocacy feels difficult, it's worth considering how early experiences may have shaped this challenge.

Remember: even if others fall short, you need to stand up for yourself. The key is to consistently remind yourself of what's reasonable. Imagine if a friend asked for the same thing. Would you see them as needy, or would you simply recognize that they were asking for something basic and deserving?

COMMUNICATING CLEARLY AND ASSERTIVELY

Self-advocacy isn't just about speaking up; it's about *how* you communicate. Being assertive means expressing your needs clearly and confidently while respecting others. It's the balance between being passive (staying silent) and aggressive (being overly forceful).

Here's how assertive communication compares to other styles:

Assertive: Clear, direct, and respectful. Uses "I"

statements. "I need more time to complete this project. Can we discuss a deadline extension?"

Passive: Avoids expressing needs, lacks confidence. "I guess I'll just try to finish it on time, even though I probably won't be able to."

Aggressive: Demands without respect for others. Blaming or hostile. "You never give me enough time! This deadline is ridiculous!"

Passive-Aggressive: Indirect, sarcastic, avoids confrontation. "Wow, guess I'll just pull an all-nighter again since deadlines are never fair."

Assertive communication is important because it allows you to stand up for yourself while respecting others, but it can be easier said than done, and it's a skill that takes time to build. Instead of seeing self-advocacy as a confrontation, view it as a constructive conversation. When you focus on your needs and how addressing them will benefit both you and others, it can feel less like an attack and more like a productive exchange.

Personally, I've had moments where my message came across stronger than I intended, which made for awkward situations. But with practice, it has gotten easier and more natural.

Here are a few tips:

- **Assume positive intent:** Most people want to be heard and understood.
- **Stay focused on your goal:** If the conversation drifts, gently steer it back.
- **Practice:** Talk to yourself, write things out, or practice with a friend.
- **Reflect on past conversations:** Think about what you wish you'd said and practice.
- **Celebrate wins:** Acknowledge your progress, no matter how small.

Like any skill, assertive communication gets easier with practice. But you'll likely have some blunders on the way. The important thing is that you are trying. And remember, just because you're focused on being assertive and constructive doesn't mean others will respond in kind. In these situations, it's helpful to assume the best while continuing to prioritize your needs and rights—even if the response you're getting isn't ideal.

OVERCOMING BARRIERS TO SELF-ADVOCACY

Understanding your rights is one thing; finding the courage to stand up for them is another. Let's look at the common barriers that might be holding you back from advocating for yourself:

Fear of Confrontation: A lot of people avoid speaking up because they fear conflict or upsetting others. The key here is to start small. Try expressing a simple need or saying "no" without overexplaining. These small steps will help you build confidence for the bigger conversations.

Self-Doubt: You might question whether your needs are worth advocating for or wonder if you have the right to speak up. Your needs matter, and they're just as valid as anyone else's. Remind yourself that you have the right to express yourself honestly, and seek support when you need it. Confidence builds over time, so give yourself grace and keep practicing.

Fear of Failure: It's natural to fear that your efforts won't work, but remember: every attempt is a step forward. Advocating for yourself is a skill, and like any skill, it gets easier the more you practice. Even when things don't go as planned, you're building resilience and learning.

Lack of Knowledge: Sometimes we avoid advocating for ourselves simply because we don't know how to do it. The more you understand your rights and how to express your needs, the more confident you'll feel. Take the time to educate yourself, whether it's researching workplace policies or learning more about your personal rights.

Fear of Not Being Liked: Prioritizing other people's opinions and being overly concerned with being liked creates an internal conflict when it's time to speak up. Remember, your needs and voice matter just as much as anyone else's. People will respect you more when you assert yourself with kindness and confidence, and those who matter will value your authenticity over the facade of being overly agreeable.

Overcoming barriers with confidence is one of the most challenging yet empowering aspects of self-advocacy. You're taught the limiting belief to "go big or go home," but sometimes, the seemingly small acts, like speaking up in a meeting or replaying how you wish you would have responded, are actually the biggest steps forward. Practice advocating for yourself through everyday actions, like asking for clarification or making a minor request. And celebrate these wins, because, with time, they will help you gain the confidence to tackle bigger challenges.

KNOWING WHERE YOUR RESPONSIBILITY ENDS

A lot of us were given false promises. We were told that if we follow a certain path, success and fulfillment will naturally follow. But when reality doesn't match those expectations, frustration builds, and responsibility is often misplaced.

Take landlords, for example. Many are sold the idea that owning rental properties is an easy way to get rich. The focus is on passive income, while the ongoing responsibilities of home maintenance, unexpected costs, and tenant needs are often ignored. When landlords don't see the big returns they expected and realize it's not as effortless as they were led to believe, frustration sets in, and many feel cheated. Meanwhile, tenants are left in homes that need repairs, often forced to advocate for basic living conditions.

A similar dynamic plays out in relationships. Society teaches us that we're entitled to a perfect partner who will meet all our needs effortlessly. When that doesn't happen, and the idealized version of a partner doesn't materialize, frustration turns into resentment. This is why we see so many men claiming to hate women and women saying "men are trash," or that they'd be better off without them. It's not the people they hate. It's the false ideas they were sold.

These societal narratives play out in many areas of life. When things don't go as expected, instead of adjusting expectations or questioning the system, people often look for someone to blame. The burden of fixing things too often falls on those who were never responsible for the problem in the first place.

While this might explain a person's actions, it doesn't excuse them, and someone else's frustration isn't yours to carry. You're responsible for your actions, your words, and those who are truly dependent on you, like children. You're not responsible for anyone else's happiness, choices, or behavior. If someone says, "You made me do that," unless coercion or power imbalances are at play, they're shifting blame. No one can truly make another person act a certain way. Try changing someone's political opinion online, and you'll see exactly what I mean.

This is why, at times, self-advocacy can feel exhausting. Not only are you standing up for yourself, you're also often pushing back against deeply ingrained beliefs and broken systems. You don't have to take on the weight of fixing everything, though. While holding others accountable may feel unsettling at times, think of it as placing responsibility where it belongs. In doing so, you are actually doing others a favor. Instead of enabling them, you encourage their growth.

THE POWER AND REALITY OF SELF-ADVOCACY

Self-advocacy is an important skill that will benefit you throughout your life. No one will fight for you the way you can fight for yourself. I wish you didn't have to fight for basic rights, but unfortunately, that's the reality for many people.

Another hard truth is that even when you advocate for yourself, your rights may still be ignored. Some workers report harassment and get dismissed. Some tenants fight unfair evictions and still lose their homes. Standing up for yourself doesn't guarantee success, but that doesn't mean it's not worth doing.

You are taught to automatically trust certain people, like doctors, employers, or those in authority, but self-advocacy reminds you that you need to trust yourself first. Questioning decisions, asking for clarification, and making informed choices are not acts of defiance—they are acts of self-respect.

Every time you push back against injustice, you create pressure for change. And even if the outcome isn't what you hoped for, self-advocacy strengthens your confidence and self-worth.

From: Disputes at PPA
To: Lyndsey Getty

Online Dispute Confirmation Ticket Number 00000

--- External Email ---

Dear Lyndsey, Your dispute will be reviewed and
investigated as requested below:

This spot is usually open when I park, and I have been using
it frequently without receiving a ticket. The street has white
boxes with an "X" painted inside, which indicate no parking.
When I received the tickets I was parked in the white box
without an "X," which a reasonable person would assume is a
legal parking space (See picture 1). The signage confusion
comes from a "No Parking - Bus Turns" sign on a pole near
the space. (Pictures 1, 2, 3 & 5). Since this is the only pole in
the area and it was pointed towards the marked "x" boxes, I
assumed the sign referred to the marked "X" boxes, not the
open white box where I parked. I believe this is a reasonable
interpretation, and my past months of parking here without
issue reinforced that belief. I request that these tickets be
removed due to the confusing signage. I also suggest moving
the "No Parking - Bus Turns" sign to the edge of the "X" box
or extending the painted markings to prevent further
confusion (picture 5). I appreciate your consideration in
resolving this issue.

[EDITED FOR BREVITY]

This is a real example of a dispute I submitted to the Philadelphia
Parking Authority (PPA) for tickets I received due to confusing
signage. In this case, I genuinely believe the tickets were
unwarranted, so I needed to advocate for myself. I took pictures,
outlined the confusion, explained what I thought was reasonable, and
suggested a long-term solution to advocate for others and prevent
similar issues in the future. The last ticket I received was almost 10
years ago. I disputed it, and it was revoked. As of now, I haven't
received a response to this one (I submitted it yesterday).

RULE #2: I DEFINE SUCCESS

In 1954, English runner Roger Bannister became the first person to run a mile in under four minutes—something that had been considered impossible. Experts thought it was a physical limitation of the human body. But once Bannister shattered the record, other runners started breaking the barrier too. Nothing had changed physically. The only thing that shifted was belief.

Success works the same way. Many of the limits you accept as unchangeable are just assumptions waiting to be broken. You're often told what success should look like, what milestones to hit, what path to follow, but those rules are not universal truths.

Bannister's story reminds us that redefining success isn't about working harder within someone else's framework. It's about rewriting the rules entirely.

WHAT DOES SUCCESS REALLY MEAN?

From the time we're kids, we're given an unspoken checklist:

- Get good grades (bonus points if you go Ivy League)
- Pick a "practical" career (that pays well immediately)
- Find the right partner (make sure they are aesthetically pleasing and rich)
- Have kids (not just one, and make sure you're a perfect parent)
- Buy a house (but don't take too long deciding)
- Work hard, retire—and then, finally, relax

These milestones aren't inherently bad, but they were never meant to define success for everyone. Yet many of us feel pressure to follow them without asking: Does this actually work for me?

Thinking big means recognizing that someone else's "key" to success may not be yours, and that's okay. For one person, success means starting a business. For another, it's having a steady nine-to-five with predictable hours. Some people thrive on adventure; others love routine. None of these are more "right" than the others—the only wrong choice is chasing a version of success that doesn't align with what you actually want.

Blindly following societal definitions of success leads to depression, a lack of purpose and fulfillment. When you realize you've been treating suggested milestones as facts rather than arbitrary recommendations, you start to question what true success looks like for you.

Now let's talk about some things that might get in the way while you redefine success.

SUCCESS BLOCKERS

Redefining success to fit your terms is empowering, but when you start making changes, doubts can creep in. Here are the biggest barriers and how to work through them.

1. PERFECTIONISM

We've been taught that success means getting it right, but in reality, success is just the result of repeated, imperfect attempts.

Maybe you hesitate to date or pursue something new because you think you'll be bad at it. Or you sit on a creative project for months because it's not "perfect." Sure, there's a possibility your first few attempts won't be good. But you need to put yourself out there to learn and grow so you can be great.

Perfectionism keeps you stuck waiting for the right moment, a time when you feel fully prepared, but that moment will never come because the right moment is whenever you decide to start.

I used to struggle with this myself. Even while writing this book, I caught myself thinking, *What if there's a typo?* But if I let that fear stop me, I wouldn't be here doing what I love. Sometimes, "good enough" has to be enough.

Overcome perfectionism by:

- Speaking up in meetings even when you're nervous.
- Applying for opportunities even if you don't meet 100% of the qualifications.
- Sharing your work before it feels "perfect" (because it never will be).
- Reminding yourself daily: *My best is enough.*

2. THINKING WITHOUT DOING

Entertaining a big idea—switching careers, starting a project, moving to a new city—feels like progress. And visualization is important, but at some point, you have to stop thinking and start doing.

Say you're considering a career change. At first, simply imagining it feels like progress (and it can be). But if weeks pass and you haven't updated your resume or followed through on a plan, then you're stuck in a cycle of inaction. The key is to move forward even when you don't feel fully ready.

Push through inaction by:

- Notice what you complain about most and take steps to improve it.
- Make the first move—schedule the meeting, sign up for the class.
- Break big goals into small steps—start by researching three job openings instead of trying to change careers overnight.
- Ask yourself: "*What's one small step I can take today that my future self will thank me for?*"

3. FEAR OF JUDGMENT AND EXTERNAL EXPECTATIONS

Choosing your own definition of success often means going against what others expect and disappointing those who want you to follow a certain path.

Maybe you want to start a business, and people say, *That's risky.* Maybe you want to leave a stable job for something more fulfilling, and they say, *Just be grateful you have a job.*

People will always have opinions, especially when you take a path they wouldn't choose themselves. But they don't have to live with your choices. You do. And if you follow someone else's advice and it doesn't work out, you won't be hard on them—you'll blame yourself.[1]

How to tune out the noise:

- Notice who's giving advice. Are they living the kind of life you want? If not, don't give their words more weight than they deserve.

- Practice a simple response to negativity: "This is the right choice for me."
- Surround yourself with people who support your version of success, not just the conventional one.
- Ask yourself: "Do I actually want this, or do I just think I should?" "If no one else's opinion mattered, what would success look like for me?"

4. DISCOMFORT

Even when you don't like where you are, it's still familiar, and familiar feels safe. That's why people stay in jobs they hate or relationships that no longer work. Growth rarely happens when you stay in your comfort zone, and redefining success requires stepping outside it. The key is to be comfortable being uncomfortable, which is easier said than done!

Steps to move past discomfort:

- Remind yourself of past times you adapted. You've done it before, you can do it again.
- Give yourself permission to feel uncomfortable and remind yourself that change feels awkward at first.
- Practice future-thinking and focus on how good it will feel to accomplish your goals.
- Ask yourself: "What's the worst that could happen?" Most fears shrink when you break them down.

5. FEELING UNWORTHY

Growing up in a dysfunctional family, I was constantly told I wouldn't amount to anything. I was repeatedly reminded I wasn't good enough and destined to fail. In a way, my success felt like I was letting my family down. When I started dreaming of speaking and writing books, part of me thought, "Who are you to want this?"

Feeling unworthy can look like doubting your dreams, questioning your right to pursue what excites you, or thinking your success would somehow be a betrayal. It's the voice inside that tells you you're not deserving, even though your heart knows better.

How to let in feelings of worthiness:

- Recognize that feeling unworthy is not a reflection of your true value.
- Speak to yourself the way you would speak to a friend going through a tough time.
- Build a network of people who encourage and believe in you.
- Focus on your strengths and what you do well.

6. COMPARISON

"Imitation is the sincerest form of flattery" means that copying another person's actions, style, or ideas shows admiration for them. It's a limiting belief.

The full version, "Imitation is the sincerest form of flattery that mediocrity can pay to greatness," provides a different perspective. It suggests that less original or talented people often imitate those who are truly great instead of creating something unique.

Using others as inspiration can be helpful, but when comparison leads to feeling behind, it becomes a roadblock. Someone else's success doesn't mean you're failing or falling behind. Often, what seems like "overnight success" is really years of unseen effort.

How to escape the comparison trap:

- Trust that things will happen for you on the right timeline.
- Strive to be genuinely happy for other people's success and use it as motivation.
- Remember, comparison is best used as a tool to help you identify what you do and don't want.
- Ask yourself: "What can I do today to help me achieve my goals tomorrow?"

7. IMAGINARY TIMELINES

Society loves a checklist: Graduate by 22, have a career by 25, buy a house by 30. But life doesn't always follow that path. Some people find success early; others take years of trial and error. Some people build careers in their twenties; others start over at 40.

There are even timelines for healing, like being told it takes half the time you were in a relationship to process it. But there's no right time for anything—only what's right for *you*.

Moving past trivial timelines:

- View timelines as flexible guidelines, not strict deadlines.
- Set flexible goals that can be adjusted over time.
- Reaffirm: There's no universal path or set schedule for success.
- Ask yourself: "Who set these expectations? Are they serving my growth, or limiting it?"

FINAL THOUGHTS ON SUCCESS

Redefining success doesn't mean throwing away milestones you once wanted to pursue. It means choosing your own path, rather than blindly following someone else's. It's not just about rejecting external expectations; it's about owning your choices, whether or not they align with the norm.

The life you want might not look like the one you were told to build—and that's totally okay.

Cambridge Dictionary defines success as "the achievement of the results wanted or hoped for."[2] Ask yourself: What are you hoping for? To measure up to trivial social standards, or are you striving to find and follow a path to a life full of purpose and fulfillment?

RULE #3: I DEFINE MY IDENTITY

Success is what you do; identity is who you are. And we spend far too much time confusing the two.

You're taught to define yourself by your achievements and by labels like:

- Jobs (e.g., I'm a lawyer, a writer, or a teacher)
- Relationships (e.g., I'm a parent, a partner, or a sibling)
- Pasts (e.g., I'm the one who always plays it safe or the one who takes risks)

But what happens when one of those labels no longer fits?

Maybe you leave a career you thought defined you, a relationship ends, or you outgrow an old version of yourself. If your identity is too tied to any one thing, losing it can feel like losing yourself. If your sense of self is tied to being the overachiever, the responsible one, or the successful one, shifting paths can feel like losing part of your identity. That's why thinking big is knowing your identity is allowed to evolve, in fact, it is meant to.

IDENTITY IS MEANT TO BE FLUID

We like certainty. It's easier to put ourselves in a box and say, "This is who I am," than to admit that we might change. But a fixed identity is a fragile one. If you define yourself by one thing, a job, a role, or a personality trait, what happens when that thing shifts?

Growth isn't just possible; it's necessary. Life forces change, whether you like it or not. Skills evolve, relationships change, and perspectives grow. If your identity is rigid, every change feels like a threat. But when you see identity as fluid, change isn't a crisis—it's an expansion.

Think about how much you've already changed. The things that once defined you, your teenage ambitions, your college mindset, or the way you saw yourself five years ago, aren't the same today. That is not a failure. That is proof of growth. Holding onto a past version of yourself just because it's familiar limits who you could become.

A fluid identity means giving yourself permission to outgrow past versions of yourself. It means understanding that learning something new doesn't mean you were wrong before. It just means you have expanded your understanding. And if you believed something and later realized you were wrong, it's not a failure or a flaw in your character. It's a sign of growth. Being wrong isn't a weakness; refusing to accept and correct it is. Changing your mind, your priorities, or your path doesn't make you lost. It makes you adaptable.

Thinking big means seeing yourself as someone in motion, not stuck in place. Instead of asking, "Who am I?" as if there's one final answer, ask, "Who am I becoming?" The most successful, fulfilled people aren't the ones who hold onto old labels; they're the ones willing to evolve.

FINDING THE IDENTITY THAT FITS

When you look at successful people, it's easy to assume they've always had it figured out. You see them at their peak and assume they always knew exactly who they were. But that's not the case. What you're seeing is the version of them that finally aligned with their growth, the result of years of trial, error, and reinvention.

Success stories are often told in hindsight. You rarely see the missteps, the doubts, or the pivots along the way. But if you look closer, you'll find people who, like you, had to let go of old identities to step into something new.

Maya Angelou didn't start as a world-renowned writer. She was a dancer, singer, cook, streetcar conductor, and civil rights activist before finding the path that fit. Each phase shaped her, and she never forced herself to stay in just one lane.

Steve Buscemi was a firefighter before becoming an actor. Acting started as a side pursuit, but when the opportunity came, he embraced it. Even after Hollywood success, he never erased his past. After 9/11, he returned to his firehouse to help. Your past doesn't have to limit you. It can expand you.

Vera Wang dreamed of becoming an Olympic figure skater. When that didn't happen, she became a journalist, then an editor at Vogue. She didn't design her first dress until her 40s. If she'd clung to her old identities, she never would have become one of the world's most influential designers.

Samuel L. Jackson struggled with addiction and small acting roles for years. He almost quit before landing his breakout role in his 40s. If you think it's too late to change or succeed, his story proves otherwise. Success is not about a perfect plan. It's about staying open to reinvention.

Harland Sanders (Colonel Sanders) worked as a farmhand, streetcar conductor, and insurance salesman before founding KFC in his 60s. His story proves that your first, second, or even third career doesn't have to be your final one.

These people were not born into the identities that made them successful. They adapted, took risks, and let go of what no longer fit. If you're holding onto an identity that feels limiting, know that you're allowed to change. Reinvention is not failure. It's growth.

Before I started writing books, I worked in tech, specializing in data privacy. I spent years negotiating agreements and writing terms and conditions most people scroll past when using a new app. It suited me for a while, and I loved negotiating. But I kept coming back to psychology and growth.

I was constantly reading, learning, and developing my own method. I thought about writing a book, and it took me ten years to finally take the leap. Letting go of my old identity wasn't easy, and I still miss it sometimes. But it wasn't about leaving something behind; it was about stepping into what fit me best.

You can start finding an identity that fits by shifting from an external to an internal one.

INTERNAL IDENTITY IS POWER

You're taught to define yourself by external factors: your appearance, job, or relationship status. But true fulfillment comes from knowing who you are on the inside. To discover your identity beyond superficial labels, you need to shift your focus to what truly matters to you.

Instead of relying on external validation, embracing an internal identity allows you to build a sense of self based on your values, passions, and personal growth. Here's the difference:

EXTERNAL IDENTITY	INTERNAL IDENTITY
Built on societal expectations and validation	Rooted in personal values and beliefs
Influenced by trends and other people's opinions	Aligned with passions, skills, and goals
Dependent on approval and recognition	Self-validated and fulfilling
Defined by wealth, status, or achievements	Guided by authenticity and individuality
Conforms to social pressure	Driven by growth, purpose, and satisfaction

Shifting from an external to an internal identity can feel overwhelming, especially if you're not sure what your true goals and passions are (no worries, I've been there). A great way to find a center is by focusing on what you value. Consider the traits below.

Kind | Considerate | Resilient | Courageous
Honest | Compassionate | Generous | Creative
Independent | Confident | Authentic | Empathetic
Determined | Adaptable | Disciplined | Optimistic
Loyal | Patient | Humble | Open-minded

What traits resonate with you most. Why?

_____

_____

_____

_____

_____

_____

AN ACTIVE CHOICE

It's not just about identifying these qualities, it's about living them. If you value honesty, be truthful, even when it's uncomfortable. If you value kindness, find small ways to show it (to yourself and others). And if all of this feels overwhelming, know that you are more courageous and resilient than you think. Working through limiting beliefs and challenging old mindsets may feel daunting, but it's an incredible act of bravery. Learning, growing, and reshaping your mindset makes you a badass.

Beyond identifying the characteristics you value, embrace your inner identity by asking yourself:

- If money weren't a factor, what would I want to do?
- What excites me?
- What do I believe, regardless of what others think?
- Do I really want to be defined by my career, a political belief, or someone else's expectations?

You don't need to have all the answers right now, but keep reflecting on these questions. Next time you're bored, instead of scrolling through social media, grabbing a beer, online shopping, or gossiping, revisit them. And hey, I'm following the Blake Lively and Justin Baldoni drama too—don't feel guilty about your lighthearted escapes. Just make sure you practice healthy moderation.

"YA BASIC" —ELEANOR SHELLSTROP

Thinking big also means owning what you truly want, even if it's considered "simple." If your dream life is a steady job, a cozy home, and weekend brunches with friends, that's just as valid as any "extraordinary" ambition. You don't have to chase someone else's dream to prove your worth. And not every moment needs to be Instagram worthy to prove you're "living your best life."

I *love* being basic. Give me a *Gilmore Girls* rerun, a solid Pilates class, and a cup of black coffee, and I'm happy. While I don't like pumpkin-flavored things, I envy people who get excited about pumpkin spice lattes every fall. They have a built-in source of joy every year, and I think that's great—even if I don't personally get it.

Thinking big isn't about rejecting the ordinary. It's about making sure your choices are *yours*, not dictated by what's trendy, expected, or "impressive" to others. It's also about following the trends you like while ditching the ones you don't. I love cozy, oversized sweaters, and like many other millennials, you'll have to pry my leggings out of my cold, dead hands. But you won't catch me waxing my eyebrows thin again (I'm grateful they grew back the first time), and bell bottoms just aren't my thing (even with Kendrick pulling them off).

Thinking big is also about embracing your own prefer-ences without putting down someone else's. So what if your neighbor puts up their Christmas lights in October? As long as they aren't shining directly into your bedroom and disrupting your sleep, how is it really affecting you? If you're bothered, it's likely less about the decorations and more about your unhealthy need for control (no judgment; I've been there more times than I would like to admit!).

And let's be real here: whom people choose to love or marry isn't your business. Unless it's someone you're romantically involved with or married to, or unless it involves a vulnerable individual, people's relationships are their choices, and whom they love doesn't affect your life unless you let it.

A common limiting belief is the idea that you need to "let" others live their lives. But thinking big isn't about "letting" others do anything. It's about realizing that you have no control over them in the first place.

If you feel the need to "let" someone do something, it's worth asking yourself why you're focusing on controlling others instead of prioritizing your own life and happiness —likely because you've been encouraged to do so by unhealthy influences.

Real identity isn't about clinging to old labels or worrying about how others live. It's about staying open to growth, making choices that align with who you are, and letting go of external validation. When you stop fearing change, you stop seeing it as loss. You start seeing it as becoming more of who you were always meant to be.

Remember: Unless someone is harming a vulnerable person, restricting your rights, or involved romantically with your monogamous partner, focusing on them won't add any real value to your life.

EMBRACING FLUIDITY

At the end of the day, identity isn't something you find—it's something you build. Changing it isn't easy. The sunk cost fallacy tells you that because you've invested time and effort into something, you should stick with it. Fear of change whispers that embracing something new means stepping into the unknown. Even subtle comments like, "But this is who you are," can make you second-guess yourself.

But you don't owe the world a fixed version of yourself. You're allowed to change, and it's easier than staying stuck in an identity that doesn't fit. You're also allowed to change your mind. People often tie their identity to beliefs, but beliefs don't define you. It's not "I think, therefore I am." It's "I think, therefore I observe."

You observe, challenge, and grow past your thoughts, but you are not them. Holding on too tightly to beliefs (like left, right, conservative, progressive) boxes you in and resists necessary change. True identity is about staying open to growth, not clinging to labels or outdated ideas.

Letting go of the fear of change means seeing it as a chance to become who you were always meant to be, not losing yourself. The world will always have opinions about who you should be, but ultimately, you're the one living with your choices. So, why not make choices that align with who you truly are?

Owning your identity is a daily choice—in how you carry yourself, set boundaries, say yes or no, and show up in the world. It's not always easy, but every time you choose authenticity over conformity, you reclaim a little more of your power.

Take it one step at a time. You don't need all the answers right now—just meeting yourself where you are is progress. Embrace change, trust that you're meant to grow, and remind yourself that you're doing the best you can.

RULE #4: I AM AN ALCHEMIST

You've already started the work. You've questioned beliefs that no longer serve you. But challenging them isn't enough, you have to replace them with something stronger. That's where mental alchemy comes in.

An alchemist of beliefs takes raw experience and refines it into wisdom, turning obstacles into stepping stones. This mindset doesn't mean pretending struggles don't exist. It means recognizing that while situations can be painful or unfair, staying stuck in bitterness or self-doubt only prolongs suffering. The better alternative is to learn, grow, and use what happens as fuel for transformation.

Traditional alchemy is turning lead into gold—wouldn't that be nice? But in real life, gaining a new perspective is the true gold. Here are some examples of this process in action:

Breakup → Rediscovery: A breakup may feel like losing part of yourself, but it's also an opportunity to reconnect with your goals. Instead of thinking, *I can't live without this person,* reflect on what you appreciated and didn't appreciate in the relationship, and use that insight to guide your future connections.

Losing Your Job → Opportunity: Losing a job can feel overwhelming, but it's also a chance to consider new directions that might better align with your goals. Shift from focusing on the loss to focusing on new possibilities.

Failing at a Project or Goal → Resilience: Failure can be discouraging, but it's an important part of learning. Instead of labeling yourself a failure, recognize the effort you put in, refine your approach, and use the experience to build resilience.

Criticism or Judgment → Self-Reflection: Criticism can sting, but it's part of life. Instead of internalizing it, reflect on why it affects you and what you can learn from it. You can appreciate both the feedback and your own growth in response.

Rejection → Redirection: Rejection can be painful, but it's also a chance to grow. Instead of focusing on the sting, acknowledge the courage it took to put yourself out there and trust that something better suited for you is ahead.

Health Issues → Strength: Health struggles can feel discouraging, but they also offer a chance to practice self-care, acceptance, and resilience.

Loss of a Friend → Growth: Losing a friend is painful, but it's also an opportunity to honor the good memories while creating space for healing and new connections.

Overwhelm → Clarity: When life feels chaotic, it's a chance to take a deep breath, step back, and prioritize what truly matters.

Loneliness → Self-Discovery: Feeling lonely is difficult, but it's also an opportunity to reconnect with yourself and your desires. It can also be a stepping stone to building better communication and relationship skills.

Anger → Curiosity and Change: Anger signals repressed emotions or unmet needs. Instead of pushing it down, ask, *What is this telling me?* and *What can I do to improve this situation?*

REINFORCING THE POWER OF CHOICE

You don't always get to choose what happens to you, but you do get to choose how you respond. Every challenge presents a fork in the road: you can let it define you, or you can define *yourself* through it.

Mental alchemy isn't about invalidating your feelings. Even the most resilient people need time to process setbacks. You're allowed to feel hurt, disappointed, or exhausted. But staying stuck in those feelings for too long only reinforces limiting beliefs.

The key is realizing that you have more than one way to frame an experience. You can choose to see a situation as a lesson, an opportunity, or even just *something that happened*—nothing more, nothing less. Not everything needs to be turned into a deep revelation. Sometimes, the most freeing thing you can do is decide that an event doesn't mean anything about you and simply move on.

When you practice alchemy, you acknowledge your emotions while choosing to move forward. You shift from *Why did this happen to me?* to *What can I create from this?* or even *Does this need to mean anything at all?*

MAKING ALCHEMY A HABIT

Mental alchemy isn't a one-time shift—it's a practice. The more you engage with it, the more natural it becomes. Here's how to integrate it into daily life:

- **ICE Limiting Beliefs:** When you notice a limiting belief, challenge and reframe it. Identify where it came from, question its validity, and choose a perspective that serves you.
- **Seek the Lesson—or Not:** Not everything carries a deep meaning. Some experiences are just that—experiences. When faced with a

challenge, ask yourself: *Is there something to learn here?* If so, use it as fuel for growth. If not, then the lesson is simply acceptance and moving forward.

- **Reinforce with Action:** A shift in perspective is powerful, but true transformation happens when you act on it. Take small, intentional steps that reflect your new mindset. The more you practice, the more second nature it becomes.

Mental alchemists don't force feeling good all the time, they recognize they have the power to shape their experience.

Some days, you'll be the alchemist. Other days, you won't have the energy, and that's okay, too. The important part is knowing that you *always* have the choice to begin again.

ALCHEMY IN ACTION: TURNING STRUGGLE INTO STRENGTH

Mental alchemy isn't just a metaphor; many people have turned personal struggles into something extraordinary:

- **Thomas Edison** failed thousands of times before inventing the light bulb. Instead of seeing failure as defeat, he viewed each attempt as a lesson that brought him closer to success.
- **Oprah Winfrey** overcame poverty and trauma to build a media empire. Instead of letting hardship

define her, she used it as fuel to create a platform that inspires millions.

- **Lady Gaga** channeled years of bullying and personal struggles into her music, using it to inspire self-acceptance and mental health awareness.

But alchemy isn't just about well-known success stories. It's happening all around you—every day.

The confident speaker on stage wasn't always comfortable with public speaking. The friend who gives great advice once struggled to take their own (they still might!). The person who seems unshakable in the face of setbacks wasn't always that way, they learned resilience by facing challenges and choosing to grow.

Mental alchemy is the quiet persistence of the parent showing up for their kids despite exhaustion. It's the student who rewrites their self-doubt into self-belief. It's the person who, after heartbreak, chooses to love again (Proud of you, you brave little toaster!).

Transformation isn't reserved for the extraordinary. It's for anyone willing to challenge their perspective and take control of their narrative. And that means it's for you, too.

YOU ARE THE ALCHEMIST

Growth isn't comfortable. The moments that feel the hardest are often the ones that bring the biggest transformation.

If you just went through a breakup, you might think you'll never find love again. If you were laid off, you might feel like you'll never find another job. Limiting beliefs make hard times even harder. But alchemists see these moments differently. Instead of focusing on what's lost, they focus on what they've learned and what they can create next.

Alchemists don't define themselves by their job, relationship, or circumstances. They know that no matter what happens, they have the power to rebuild. Some people suggest that simply thinking positively will magically bring success, but that's not how transformation works. Your thoughts influence your emotions, which shape your actions, and those actions lead to results. Change isn't instant, but when you shift your mindset, you create new opportunities.

For example, if you expect self-growth to take time, you'll feel more at ease and stay committed. But if you believe transformation must happen overnight, you'll feel frustrated and burned out. True alchemy happens when you remove the pressure and focus on steady, sustainable progress.

Sometimes life makes you feel like you've had to be too strong. You've been through things that didn't kill you, but damn, they definitely left their mark. It sucks. And I'm sorry it's this way. But when you become an alchemist, you learn to do the best you can with the situation you have. And that's valid.

It's also okay to say, *"I'm an alchemist... but not today."* Sometimes, the most powerful thing you can do is give yourself permission to rest. Real transformation happens when you balance effort with recovery. You're allowed to take your time, that's part of the alchemical process too.

Remember: the gold you're searching for? It's already within you. (I know this might sound cliché, but it's absolutely true.)

RULE #5: I AM NOT ALONE

In recent years, a massive shift has taken place. As society reduces the stigma surrounding mental health, more people are openly discussing anxiety, depression, self-doubt, and intrusive thoughts. Conversations that were once whispered behind closed doors are now happening openly, reminding us that we don't have to suffer in silence.

However, despite this progress, the deeply ingrained message that we must face our battles alone still lingers. Many people struggle with the limiting belief that their pain is unique, that no one could possibly understand their struggles. This isolates us, convincing us to stay quiet for fear of judgment or misunderstanding. It's a trick our minds play on us, reinforced by societal conditioning to keep our struggles hidden.

Thinking big means recognizing that, even in moments of solitude, you're never truly alone. Across the world, countless others are navigating their own challenges, striving to grow, and seeking connection.

When you embrace this truth, you stop seeing struggle as something that separates you from others and start seeing it as something that brings us together. By opening up, you invite support, understanding, and the realization that you're part of something bigger than just your individual pain. You also help remove the shame surrounding vulnerability and being human for future generations.

Let's use the ICE Method to reframe this limiting belief together.

IDENTIFYING THE LONELINESS BLOCKER

To challenge a limiting belief, we first need to recognize it. Here are some ways the isolation trap might show up in your life:

- **Feeling Unique in Struggles:** We often think our challenges are one-of-a-kind, but many share similar emotions like fear, shame, and self-doubt.
- **Hesitating to Open Up:** It's easy to think others won't understand, but the right people will listen and offer support.
- **Viewing Support as Weakness:** Asking for help isn't weakness; it's a strength that creates real connection and growth.

- **Feeling Isolated Among Others:** Loneliness can happen even when surrounded by people if we're not sharing our true thoughts and feelings.
- **Downplaying Struggles:** Comparing pain invalidates your own; every struggle deserves acknowledgment, regardless of others' situations.
- **Glamorizing Others:** Successful people face struggles too. Confidence and achievement often come from persistence, not magical traits.

Many of us feel alone not because no one understands us, but because we've internalized the belief that we must face challenges in isolation. Whether it's due to past experiences, judgment, or simply how we were raised, identifying these patterns is the first step toward connection.

What makes you feel isolated in your struggles? Are you assuming no one will understand? Are you holding back from connecting because of past experiences or fears?

_____

_____

_____

_____

_____

My answer: When I cut ties with my family, I faced a lot of harsh judgment. The one friend I confided in wasn't supportive, so I decided to handle things on my own. When it comes to work and success, I always assumed successful people were the "others" and had or knew something I didn't.

CHALLENGING THE ISOLATION TRAP

A woman posted a TikTok video about growing up in a non-affectionate household and struggling to accept love as an adult. Within two weeks, her video gained 7.9 million views and thousands of comments from people who shared similar experiences.[1] Her story shows that shared struggles are far more common than we realize. Sometimes, we just need to be the first to speak up and share, creating space for others to do the same.

Here are some perspectives that can help challenge the limiting belief that you're alone in our struggles:

- **The Strength of Vulnerability:** Vulnerability is a strength, allowing us to share imperfect parts of ourselves. By opening up, we make space for empathy, understanding, and deeper connections.
- **Social Media as Connection:** While social media has its downsides, it can also offer communities where we share struggles and find reassurance that we're not alone.
- **Bravery in Seeking Support:** Reaching out for support can be daunting, but it's an act of bravery that reminds us we're not alone. Whether through friends, therapy, or online groups, asking for help is empowering.

- **Strength in Admitting Fear:** Admitting fear or nervousness builds trust and invites connection with others who can relate to your experiences.

Did anyone—family, teachers, or the media—suggest, directly or indirectly, that you shouldn't share your struggles? Is that assumption true? Can you think of a time when someone else shared a similar experience, helping you realize you weren't as isolated as you thought?

_____

_____

_____

_____

_____

My answer: Seeing people share their stories of leaving dysfunctional families on social media has helped me feel connected. While I wish no one had to make that choice, each story reminds me that others are going through similar things. As far as work and success, I know the true power is in persistence and consistency.

EVALUATE – IS THIS BELIEF HELPING OR HURTING YOU?

Challenging the belief that we're alone in our struggles opens us to new perspectives. But simply recognizing that the belief is limiting isn't enough to change it. We need to evaluate how this shift is happening and take action.

- **Actions That Connect:** Start small by reaching out to one person or community, like a friend, an online group, or a support organization. Even small actions, such as a simple conversation or social post, reinforce that you're not alone. You can also explore resources like Brené Brown for deeper insights into vulnerability and boundaries.[2]
- **Benefits of Connection:** Realizing you're not the only one going through something makes it easier to ask for help. Listening to how others overcame challenges can offer new perspectives or reassure you things can improve. The act of opening up keeps you moving forward.
- **Obstacles to Connection:** Fear of judgment, past trauma, or negative self-talk may hold you back. Recognizing these barriers is the first step in overcoming them. It's okay to feel hesitant— facing these challenges is a gradual process, but worth it.

What small steps can you take to reach out to someone or join a community that might help you feel less isolated? How will connecting with others make it easier for you to keep moving forward or find new solutions? What are some obstacles you might face when trying to connect with others? How can you overcome them?

_____

_____

_____

My answer: *Writing can be a lonely process, but I'm taking action by joining writers' groups and working in coffee shops to feel more connected. I realize that my nervousness about trusting others holds me back, but I'm learning to be more understanding and not as hard on myself or others.*

A NEW NARRATIVE

When I was learning public speaking, I thought letting the audience know I was nervous at the beginning of my speech would help me feel more connected to them. But my coach told me not to do it, saying it would hurt my authority. It didn't feel right, but I listened. Then, I came across something the founder of TED Talks said: admitting you're nervous at the start actually helps create connection with the audience.[3] Turns out, I was right all along, and my coach was unintentionally limiting me with bad advice.

Well-intentioned coaches may advise us to project authority, and we can be influenced by the belief that showing emotions will cause others to lose respect for us. But sometimes, the best way to connect is to show vulnerability and let people in. This doesn't guarantee that people will welcome us or that we'll get the results we want, but it does mean we tried. And one of the most respectful things you can do is show up as your authentic self.

CONCLUSION: THINK. BIG.

If you feel stuck, want better relationships, a more fulfilling career, or a deeper connection with yourself, change starts with the belief system that got you where you are today. And limiting beliefs are often the first thing standing in your way. To remove these blockers, you have to continually challenge them.

Shifting from a limited mindset to an empowering one isn't impossible, but it can feel that way. Mostly because you were never taught how, and simply hearing "dream big" isn't enough to break through the limiting beliefs that have been holding you back.

If you had learned how to overcome blockers when you were a kid, it would be second nature. Now, you need to actively develop that skill while remembering that beliefs like "things should be quick, easy, and painless" will only hold you back. Societally accepted limiting beliefs about growth and progress make you feel like you're failing when you're really just going through the process. Remember: trust the process.

When you think big you take responsibility for one of the rare things you can control—your thoughts. Thinking big is being curious, asking questions when it's easier not to, wondering why things are the way they are, and not accepting "because it's always been that way" as an answer. Sure, some things are fine "as is," but I'm pretty sure we can all agree there's room for improvement.

I had to challenge a lot of limiting beliefs to create the life I wanted, and I'm still actively working through new ones I've uncovered.

Removing blockers felt like chipping away at a mountain. Slowly, I released the idea that therapy was for "losers," that emotions were weakness, and that I wasn't allowed to relax and have fun. I realized it's not lame to be your own best friend. Seriously, why wouldn't we be? I even did a power pose in my house when I learned there's no excuse for abuse. (Thanks, Lundy!)

To reach my health goals, I had to unlearn the male-centered fitness standards I'd been given, and fully commit to lifting weights and working out, even though I was told it would make me "bulky" and "too masculine." Spoiler alert: it didn't.

At the gym, I had to overcome the belief that "everyone" was watching me. A colleague once told me, "No one cares," and eventually, someone commented on my progress. That's when I learned balance: people do notice, but I get to decide if that matters.

I also found fascinating things, like how the most decorated Viking warrior was a woman, but because of limiting beliefs about gender, some scientists refused to accept this, even with DNA evidence.[1] And that women were once the primary hunters in tribes—a quiet fact buried under centuries of men telling women they were naturally submissive.[2]

I've also learned that happiness is a choice, even if it's not one we make every day.

Outdated beliefs shape the way we see ourselves and the world. The more we uncover the truth, the more we heal.

In fact, we're in a time of transformation and healing. Part of that means removing blockers that no longer serve us.

If you've ever felt overwhelmed by how much needs to change, remember this: by starting small, you're thinking big. It may seem like it takes a lot of people to make an impact, but one voice can be powerful enough to shift the course of history (imagine how much damage Descartes did).

Pointing out limiting beliefs can be uncomfortable, but it gets easier. It's easy to forget that what you see on social media isn't real life, and we need to constantly remind ourselves of this. And when you start to think in a more empowered way, not everyone will understand; some may even try to tear you down, but that's their struggle, not yours.

One of the biggest lessons we can learn is that our opinion of ourselves matters most. We can't control what others think about us—we've been sold a losing game. And yet, we often try to force our beliefs onto others, assuming that what worked for us is the only path. But true leadership doesn't come from force; it comes from living fully and authentically so others feel inspired to do the same.

Other authors have given me a sense of connection and joy through this process, and I hope I've done the same for you. I know it's easy to feel like everyone has a hidden agenda. I've done my best to be unbiased, non-religious, and non-political. I've tried to use a variety of examples so you will feel seen and heard. And while I didn't cover every limiting belief, I hope I gave you a solid place to start.

Mr. Rogers told us to "look for the helpers." This doesn't just mean people helping through actions; it's also about those with empowering mindsets. Look for the people who are thinking big, challenging limits, and inspiring change. And most importantly, know that you already are that person.

Be good. Think big. Love ya!

POWER POSE

1. **Stand Tall:** Feet shoulder-width apart, spine straight, shoulders back.
2. **Open Up:** Take up space; don't cross arms or hunch over.
3. **Choose a Pose:**
   - **Wonder Woman:** Hands on hips, chin up.
   - **Victory Pose:** Arms raised in a "V" shape.
   - **CEO Pose:** Hands on a table, leaning slightly forward.
4. **Hold for 2 Minutes:** Breathe deeply, think confident thoughts.
5. **Release and Walk with Purpose:** Carry the confidence with you.

TEMPLATES

ICE METHOD

Situation Nickname: _____

Identify
Describe the situation. Write down as many details as you can. What limiting beliefs are you noticing? Can you identify where these beliefs originated from? Are there specific phrases or patterns in your internal dialogue that reinforce these beliefs?

_____

_____

_____

_____

_____

_____

Challenge
Are you making assumptions? Do you have any facts to support your beliefs? What are some more expansive or empowering thoughts you could adopt? What would you say to a friend if they were in the same situation?

_____

_____

_____

_____

_____

_____

Evaluate

How will replacing this limiting belief with a more
empowering one help you reach your goals? What
actions can you take to move past this belief? What's
holding you back from making a change?

_____

_____

_____

_____

_____

_____

NOTES:

ICE METHOD

Situation Nickname: _____

Identify
Describe the situation. Write down as many details as you can. What limiting beliefs are you noticing? Can you identify where these beliefs originated from? Are there specific phrases or patterns in your internal dialogue that reinforce these beliefs?

_____

_____

_____

_____

_____

_____

Challenge
Are you making assumptions? Do you have any facts to support your beliefs? What are some more expansive or empowering thoughts you could adopt? What would you say to a friend if they were in the same situation?

_____

_____

_____

_____

_____

_____

Evaluate

How will replacing this limiting belief with a more
empowering one help you reach your goals? What
actions can you take to move past this belief? What's
holding you back from making a change?

_____

_____

_____

_____

_____

_____

NOTES:

ICE METHOD

Situation Nickname: _____

Identify
Describe the situation. Write down as many details as you can. What limiting beliefs are you noticing? Can you identify where these beliefs originated from? Are there specific phrases or patterns in your internal dialogue that reinforce these beliefs?

_____

_____

_____

_____

_____

_____

Challenge
Are you making assumptions? Do you have any facts to support your beliefs? What are some more expansive or empowering thoughts you could adopt? What would you say to a friend if they were in the same situation?

_____

_____

_____

_____

_____

_____

Evaluate

How will replacing this limiting belief with a more
empowering one help you reach your goals? What
actions can you take to move past this belief? What's
holding you back from making a change?

_____

_____

_____

_____

_____

_____

_____

NOTES:

ICE METHOD

Situation Nickname: _____

Identify
Describe the situation. Write down as many details as you can. What limiting beliefs are you noticing? Can you identify where these beliefs originated from? Are there specific phrases or patterns in your internal dialogue that reinforce these beliefs?

_____

_____

_____

_____

_____

_____

Challenge
Are you making assumptions? Do you have any facts to support your beliefs? What are some more expansive or empowering thoughts you could adopt? What would you say to a friend if they were in the same situation?

_____

_____

_____

_____

_____

_____

Evaluate

How will replacing this limiting belief with a more
empowering one help you reach your goals? What
actions can you take to move past this belief? What's
holding you back from making a change?

_____

_____

_____

_____

_____

_____

NOTES:

ICE METHOD

Situation Nickname: _____

Identify
Describe the situation. Write down as many details as you can. What limiting beliefs are you noticing? Can you identify where these beliefs originated from? Are there specific phrases or patterns in your internal dialogue that reinforce these beliefs?

_____

_____

_____

_____

_____

_____

Challenge
Are you making assumptions? Do you have any facts to support your beliefs? What are some more expansive or empowering thoughts you could adopt? What would you say to a friend if they were in the same situation?

_____

_____

_____

_____

_____

_____

Evaluate

How will replacing this limiting belief with a more
empowering one help you reach your goals? What
actions can you take to move past this belief? What's
holding you back from making a change?

_____

_____

_____

_____

_____

_____

NOTES:

NOTES

TAUGHT TO BE SMALL

1. Her ex-husband, Liam Hemsworth
2. At the time of writing, the measles outbreak in Texas, United States, has already claimed two young lives. Extensive scientific research has shown no link between vaccines and autism.
3. Sheldrake (1999), p. 5.
4. Hall, H. (2017, December 12). *Freud was a fraud: A triumph of pseudoscience*. Science-Based Medicine. https://sciencebasedmedicine. org/freud-was-a-fraud-a-triumph-of-pseudoscience/
5. Encyclopædia Britannica. (n.d.). *What Darwin got right—and wrong—about evolution*. Encyclopædia Britannica. https://www. britannica.com/story/what-darwin-got-right-and-wrong-about-evolution
6. Popper (1963), pp. 147-150
7. Bancroft (2003), pp. 279-280. Bancroft discusses Freud's contribution to victim-blaming and how it negatively impacts victims today. Freud originally discovered that his patients were having emotional reactions to incest, but his findings were considered controversial. In response, Freud developed the Oedipus complex, insisting that his patients were sexually attracted to their fathers, rather than acknowledging the trauma they experienced.
8. James (1914/1907), Introductory.
9. Lamott (1995), xxviii.
10. While this may explain emotional outbursts, it does not excuse them. People are responsible for their words and actions, regardless of their beliefs.
11. Morgan, R., Stock, L., & Cavanaugh, J. (1944). *You're nobody till somebody loves you* [Recorded by Dean Martin]. On *Dean Martin Hits Again*. Reprise Records.
12. Popper (1963), Preface.

SPOTTING LIMITS

1. Swartz, T. H., Palermo, A. S., Masur, S. K., & Aberg, J. A. (2019). The science and value of diversity: Closing the gaps in our understanding of inclusion and diversity. *Journal of Infectious Diseases, 220*(Suppl 2), S33–S41. https://doi.org/10.1093/infdis/jiz174

2. Le Mat, F., Géry, M., Besson, T., Ferdynus, C., Bouscaren, N., & Millet, G. Y. (2023). Running endurance in women compared to men: Retrospective analysis of matched real-world big data. *Sports Medicine, 53*(4), 917–926. https://doi.org/10.1007/s40279-023-01813-4

3. Isenberg, N., & Brauer, M. (2024). Diversity and inclusion have greater support than most Americans think. *Scientific Reports, 14*, 28616. https://doi.org/10.1038/s41598-024-76761-8

4. Phillips, K. W. (2017, September 18). How diversity makes us smarter. *Greater Good Science Center.* https://greatergood.berkeley.edu/article/item/how_diversity_makes_us_smarter

5. Kerr, J. M. (2023, June 20). Can people really change who they are? *Psychology Today.* https://www.psychologytoday.com/us/blog/indispensable-thinking/202306/can-people-really-change-who-they-are

BREAKING THE BOX

1. Baughman, F. (2006). There is no such thing as a psychiatric disorder/disease/chemical imbalance. *PLoS Medicine, 3*(7), e318. https://doi.org/10.1371/journal.pmed.0030318

2. Robson, D. (2019, May 13). The '3.5% rule': How a small minority can change the world. *BBC Future.* https://www.bbc.com/future/article/20190513-it-only-takes-35-of-people-to-change-the-world

3. Le Texier, T. (2018). *Histoire d'un mensonge: enquête sur l'expérience de Stanford [The history of a lie]* (in French). Zones.

VIEW FROM THE TOP

1. Fryer, R. G., Jr. (2019). An empirical analysis of racial differences in police use of force. *Journal of Political Economy, 127*(3), 1210–1261. https://doi.org/10.1086/701423

RULE #2: I DEFINE SUCCESS

1. Hartigan, H. (2025, February 27). Going against one's better judgment amplifies self-blame. *Cornell Chronicle*. https://news.cornell.edu/stories/2025/02/going-against-ones-better-judgment-amplifies-self-blame

2. Cambridge University Press. (n.d.). *Success*. In *Cambridge Dictionary*. Retrieved March 12, 2025, from https://dictionary.cambridge.org/us/dictionary/english/success

RULE #5: I AM NOT ALONE

1. People. (2023, February 7). *Woman's post on struggling to be affectionate with her kids goes viral*. People. https://people.com/womans-post-on-struggling-to-be-affectionate-with-her-kids-goes-viral-8787829?utm_source=chatgpt.com

2. Brown, B. (2010, June). *The power of vulnerability* [Video]. TEDx. https://www.ted.com/talks/brene_brown_the_power_of_vulnerability

3. Abrahams, M. (2018, April). *Speaking up without freaking out* [Video]. TEDxPaloAlto.

CONCLUSION: THINK. BIG.

1. Morgan, T. (2023, October 2). DNA suggests Viking women were powerful warriors: It's the first genetic confirmation of a female Viking warrior. *History*. https://www.history.com/news/dna-proves-viking-women-were-powerful-warriors

2. Anderson, A., Chilczuk, S., Nelson, K., Ruther, R., & Wall-Scheffler, C. (2023). The myth of man the hunter: Women's contribution to the hunt across ethnographic contexts. *PLOS ONE, 18*(6), e0287101. https://doi.org/10.1371/journal.pone.0287101

REFERENCES AND FURTHER READING

To keep it conversational, I kept citations to a minimum. In the "Notes" section, you will find the online works that were cited. If you're interested in learning more, the books that were referenced, along with recommended readings, are provided below.

Bancroft, L. (2003). *Why does he do that? Inside the minds of angry and controlling men*. Penguin.

Brown, B. (2012). *Daring greatly: How the courage to be vulnerable transforms the way we live, love, parent, and lead*. Gotham Books.

Burns, D. D. (2006). *When panic attacks: The new, drug-free anxiety therapy that can change your life*. Harmony.

Dweck, C. S. (2006). *Mindset: The new psychology of success*. Random House.

Greenberger, D., & Padesky, C. A. (2015). *Mind over mood: Change how you feel by changing the way you think* (2nd ed.). Guilford Publications.

James, W. (1914). *The energies of men* (New ed.). Moffat, Yard and Company. (Original work published 1907).

Lamott, A. (1995). *Bird by bird: Some instructions on writing and life*. Anchor Books.

Popper, K. R. (1963). *The open society and its enemies* (Vol. 1). Harper & Row.

Sheldrake, R. (1999). *Dogs that know when their owners are coming home: And other unexplained powers of animals*. Three Rivers Press.

Tolle, E. (1997). *The power of now: A guide to spiritual enlightenment*. Namaste Publishing.

AUTHOR'S NOTE

The fourth book in the Thoughtbooks series, *Big Think*, had a significant impact on me. It includes examples of limiting beliefs that I've faced and those I've seen affect others. Writing this book was a powerful experience, and I hope it brings a similar sense of clarity and empowerment to you.

ACKNOWLEDGEMENTS

Thank you to those who openly share their mental health struggles and to those working to take control of their thoughts—you keep me going. To Virginia Woolf and the many women who, despite fear and opposition, wrote when the world told them not to. Thank you for lighting the way. To those who have stood up for free speech, your courage made this possible, and with these words, I honor you. To the editors and formatters who helped bring this book together. And a special thank you to my therapist and mental health professionals, whose insights continue to change lives.

Big Think

Lyndsey Getty

Thoughts Are Better Shared

A Book Club Guide

a letter to readers - edit

Hey!

My favorite part of *Big Think* is the rules. I love them so much that it's hard to pick just one.

In self-advocacy, I hope you find your voice. In defining success and identity, I hope you cut through the noise to discover your authentic self. In mental alchemy, I hope you see the pure gold in new perspectives. And in sharing struggles, I hope you feel less alone, even when you are.

More than anything, I hope *Big Think* inspires you to find the joy and love you deserve.

While I've kept things casual here, reframing limiting beliefs isn't always easy. Be kind to yourself during this process.

Thank you so much for reading, and I hope you enjoy discussing your favorite parts of the book!

-Lyndsey

discussion guidelines

These guidelines create a foundation for healthy and thoughtful discussions, while ensuring participants feel supported and respected.

1. **Confidentiality is Key.** What's said in the discussion stays in the discussion. This creates a safe space for all participants to share their thoughts and feelings openly without fear of judgment or gossip.
2. **Respect All Perspectives.** Everyone has different experiences and viewpoints. Listen actively and respectfully, even if you don't agree. Avoid interrupting and make space for others to speak.
3. **No Fixing or Advising.** Unless someone asks for advice, avoid jumping in with solutions. The goal is to share and listen, not to solve or "fix" each other's problems.
4. **Mental Health Awareness.** If someone expresses distress or seems in need of help, gently encourage them to reach out to their therapist or call a mental health hotline (such as the **Suicide & Crisis Lifeline: 988**). The book club is a space for discussion, not professional mental health support.
5. **Nonjudgmental Space.** Avoid judgmental language and tone. This includes refraining from criticizing others' thoughts, opinions, or personal experiences.

6. **Participation Is Encouraged, but Optional.**
   While everyone is encouraged to participate, it's
   okay if someone wants to pass on a question or
   doesn't feel ready to share. Participation should
   be voluntary and without pressure.
7. **Keep it Constructive.** Constructive discussions
   help us grow, while negativity can hinder open
   communication. Focus on productive, thoughtful
   sharing and be mindful of how your words
   impact others

* * *

Constructive feedback offers thoughtful and respectful
responses creating a supportive environment for discussion. It looks like:

- **Acknowledging contributions:** "I really
  appreciated your interpretation of that chapter.
  It made me think differently about the concept."
- **Offering friendly suggestions:** "Could the
  theme you mentioned be expanded by
  considering other viewpoints?"
- **Encouraging dialogue:** "What you said was
  interesting! I'd love to hear more about how you
  think that connects other areas in the book."

1. What did you know about limiting beliefs and mental blockers before reading *Big Think*?

2. How have limiting beliefs impacted your life? Will you share an example where a limiting belief held you back?

3. Reflect on the "Taught to Be Small" section of the book. Were you surprised by how many limiting beliefs or extremes are present in your surroundings? Think about the people, situations, or media you engage with daily. How do these extremes and beliefs influence your thoughts and actions? Did any specific examples from the section resonate with your experiences?

4. When learning about your mindset, where do you find yourself holding limiting beliefs the most? What steps can you take to challenge and replace these beliefs with a more empowered perspective?

5. *Big Think* discusses the importance of recognizing limiting beliefs. What are some examples of limiting beliefs you can identify in your own life, and how can you address them?

6. Can you identify a recent situation where a limiting belief influenced your thinking? What were the circumstances, and how did it affect your emotions or decisions?

7. Share a time when you successfully challenged a limiting belief in a challenging situation. How

did it change the outcome or your feelings about the situation?

8. How can focusing on long-term benefits help mitigate the feelings of failure that often come from limiting beliefs?

9. Discuss how the people around you affect your beliefs. Are there certain people who reinforce your limiting beliefs, and how can you address this?

10. What specific strategies or exercises from the book do you find most helpful for overcoming limiting beliefs? How can you integrate these into your daily routine?

11. Reflect mental alchemy. How does this idea resonate with you? How can it help you move past limiting beliefs?

12. What fears or challenges do you face when trying to overcome limiting beliefs? How can you overcome these obstacles?

13. How do you think overcoming limiting beliefs can impact society as a whole? What changes would you like to see in the way people think and approach challenges if more people learned to challenge their limiting beliefs?

RESOURCES

The information and advice in this book are not a substitute for therapeutic or medical care. Please seek professional help if you believe you may have a condition. If you or someone you care about needs support or someone to talk to, here are two key resources that can help:

Suicide & Crisis Lifeline
A free, confidential 24/7 hotline for individuals in crisis or emotional distress.
988
988lifeline.org

The National Domestic Violence Hotline
A free, confidential 24/7 hotline for anyone experiencing domestic violence or questioning their relationship.
1-800-799-SAFE (7233)
thehotline.org

ABOUT THE AUTHOR

PHOTO BY: Zave Smith

Lyndsey Getty is the creator of Thought Intelligence and founder of The Thought Method Company. She lives in Philadelphia, Pennsylvania.

thoughtmethod.com
@thoughtmethod:

Write to Us!
I'd love to hear about your experience with *Big Think* and how it has helped you (or how you think we can improve). Email me at lyndsey@thoughtmethod.com.

Your Voice Matters!
Please help others discover *Big Think* by leaving a review on Amazon. Reviews not only helps new readers but also supports indie authors like me.

For more books and updates:
thoughtmethod.com

The Thoughtbook Series

Overthink

calm
thoughts

Stop overthinking and boost confidence.
Build helpful thought patterns.
Control your thoughts.

lyndsey getty

Middle Think

balanced
thoughts

Stop all-or-nothing thinking.
Build a balanced mindset.
Overcome perfectionism.

lyndsey getty

Clear Think

clear
thoughts

Stop emotions from clouding your judgement.
Stay levelheaded under pressure.
Make smarter decisions.

lyndsey getty

Big Think

empowered
thoughts

Remove mental blockers.
Grow and unlock your potential.
Build confidence and step into your power.

lyndsey getty

Overthink: Calm Thoughts

OVERWHELMED BY CONSTANT MENTAL CHATTER? TRIED EVERYTHING TO QUIET YOUR MIND BUT NOTHING WORKS?

Overthink offers innovative strategies to help you silence mental noise and regain control of your thoughts. Instead of shutting them down, you'll learn to think in a way that truly serves you. Drawing on a decade of research and insights from hundreds of overthinkers, this practical guide explains why common advice often falls short and provides a smarter approach to calm, effective thinking.

With relatable examples and hands-on techniques, *Overthink* delivers valuable insights on every page, including:

- How your thoughts and unconscious mind work
- The unproductive thoughts that keep you stuck
- A simple three-step method to reclaim your mind
- Ways to build confidence and a growth mindset
- Practical strategies to increase your success

This isn't just about silencing your thoughts. It's about transforming them into a powerful tool for clarity, confidence, and purposeful action. *Overthink* isn't just a book; it's a roadmap to a calmer, sharper, and more empowered mind.

Middle Think: Balanced Thoughts

Middle Think

DOES YOUR MIND JUMP BETWEEN EXTREMES, PERFECTIONISM, ALL-OR-NOTHING THINKING, FEELING LIKE THINGS WON'T GET BETTER?

Middle Think offers a powerful yet simple approach to breaking free from these mental traps Instead of getting stuck in rigid thought patterns, you will learn how to embrace a balanced mindset that fosters clarity, confidence, and resilience.

With relatable examples and actionable strategies, this practical guide helps you shift from extreme thinking to a more flexible, realistic perspective. Key takeaways, include:

- How extreme thinking affects emotions, decisions, and relationships
- Practical techniques to recognize and reframe unhelpful thoughts
- Simple exercises to build mental balance and reduce stress
- Strategies to strengthen resilience and improve self-awareness
- Tools to navigate life's complexities with a clearer, steadier mindset

This is not about suppressing your thoughts, it is about transforming them. *Middle Think* gives you the tools to move beyond extremes and build a mindset that works for you, not against you.

Clear Think: Clear Thoughts

DO YOUR EMOTIONS CLOUD YOUR JUDGMENT? STRUGGLING TO STAY LEVELHEADED UNDER PRESSURE?

Clear Think offers a practical, no-nonsense approach to making better decisions, staying in control of your emotions, and thinking with confidence. Instead of letting stress and overthinking take over, you'll learn how to manage your mindset and stay clearheaded—even in high-pressure situations. With actionable strategies and relatable examples, this guide will help you:

- Separate facts from feelings to make sound decisions
- Strengthen emotional intelligence and improve self-awareness
- Build confidence by defining your boundaries and values
- Learn to respond thoughtfully instead of reacting impulsively
- Turn past mistakes into valuable opportunities for growth

You don't have to be ruled by emotions or stuck in reactive thinking. *Clear Think* gives you the tools to stay calm, focused, and in control no matter what life throws your way.

*To my daughters who helped me
get to this stage of life.*

Becoming
an
Empty Nester

Discover 50 Ideas to Enjoy
Your Next Stage of Life

PILAR KELLENBARGER

Contents

Preface

As I finish my book and prepare for its launch, I receive wonderful news. After being away for nine years, my youngest daughter is coming back home.

After spending five years on the east coast completing her MBA and then four more years working and living in Gloucester, MA with her husband, they just received orders to come live in San Diego for four years. When I heard those wonderful words, my heart burst into tears.

Because even though I practiced these fifty ideas of enjoying my empty nest, the sadness that was inside came tumbling out. What a release of tears from missing her and my other daughter.

Both daughters went out and are doing their thing by contributing to the world and finding their passion. While they did that, I practiced these ideas and learned to enjoy this new stage of my life.

As I thank the universe for helping me move through all these special moments as a mom, I see how practicing these steps helped. I truly learned to live with a positive attitude while they're off living their lives.

By taking one step and idea at a time, I wish for you to see the beauty in all your actions you took to get to this special place of your empty nest.

Introduction

As I stared out the window, I could hear my own sniffles through my thoughts. "Where did the time go? How can I be driving away with one less child in my car?" That moment that I realized I wouldn't be seeing her every day any longer; the pain started again in my heart as the tears came pouring out. As I think back, my mind starts replaying the last 10 minutes where I was holding my daughter tightly not wanting to let her go. I knew once I let her go, that would be it. After saying my goodbyes, my other daughter, my husband and I started walking towards the staircase made of old colonial gray rock hand in hand.

I remember how green the grass was and the muffled noise of groups of people talking. I looked back, but she was trying hard to focus on her new roommate and the roommate's parents. As I approached the stairs, I took one more look. I was grateful to see her give me one more glance. I sent one last air-kiss her way and descended the stairs. At the bottom, my younger daughter and husband were waiting for me. I reached out to hold their hands as we walked quietly to the car in the parking lot listening to each other's faint cries.

At least there were others with me when I took my first to college. When I became a true empty nester, I was by myself.

My youngest had selected a school back East like her sister. Because she was playing volleyball for them, she had to show up earlier for pre-season. After ten days of workouts, I returned to her college with the rest of her things. I helped move her into her permanent dorm, took her to the store to gather the last supplies needed, and then walked with her down three floors to my rental car. This time it was just me; no one else to hold onto.

As I turned to her, I put a huge mom smile on my face and started saying goodbye. As I held her tightly, it brought back the time I said goodbye to her sister just two years earlier. My mind started filling with thoughts of, How am I going to get on a plane all by myself and travel 3,000 miles from here home? Right then a mother's worst nightmare happened. My daughter pulled away from me, looked me straight in the eyes and said, "Mom, how am I gonna do this? I don't think I can do this."

Oh no, I can't believe she's saying this right now. I wanted to grab her and say, "Ok, go get your things and you can leave." But the mom who knows she's only on loan stepped up. I looked her straight in the eyes and with a calm smile I simply said, "You're going to be fine. I'm only a phone call and FaceTime away. You were born to do this. Give me a kiss. You're gonna be fine."

I smiled right into her eyes and blew her a kiss as I got into the car. A gave her a few beeps and headed out of the parking lot. I saw her turn and walk to her dorm room. That's when the flood gates opened for me. On the other hand, she didn't run after me, nor did she fall apart. I want to think that Jesus had her on one side, and her Papa had her on the other.

Thinking back on those pivotal days of my life, I truly learned how strong I am. I learned that I could do the impossible and leave my girls on the East Coast and not see them until Christmas break. I learned what it meant to be an empty nester. I knew there was going to be a lot to learn to be able to live in this new space.

Dealing with Reality

I'm writing this book to help other parents deal with this new stage of their lives. Whether your little chick-a-dees are flying the nest for college or moving into their first apartment, these fifty chapters are the different ways I dealt with the pain in order to find happiness again despite being an empty nester.

Having two children, sisters who liked to nag and pick on each other, as scholar athletes throughout high school, sometimes our family was pulled into two directions. We spent many weekends split up as a family because one daughter was at a volleyball tournament and the other was at a swim meet or water polo match.

As I approached my first daughter leaving for college, I began to hear from others how their friends were always complaining or squawking about being empty nesters. If I'm perfectly honest, I was looking forward to the quiet and the clutter free home. Because being a parent of a scholar athlete is so grueling, I was excited to part ways with the traveling every weekend day.

When I think back to both girls starting off on their own, it was nice to relax, but then the quiet became too quiet. Since I remembered that my girls were only on loan, I made a list of all the things I used to think about doing while driving to one of their tournaments.

I don't know about you, but I had a long list from riding my bike to just enjoying leafing through a magazine quietly on the couch. If I'm honest again, having one gone and learning to live that new life without the other was great practice. It somehow helped me get accustomed to the idea that one day they'll both be gone.

Here's How to Start

So before you begin reading, go get a piece of paper and jot down all the things you'd like to do now that you have more time for you. Now, thumb through my fifty short chapter ideas to help you discover the fun you can now have after all the work you put into raising your children. Take note of the ones that hit you right away, and start creating fun things to do for the next week.

After that, think of something big like a trip - somewhere you've always wanted to travel to. Bear in mind that your heart and first thought may be towards the city where your child now lives. If so, find something near them that you always wanted to visit or see. Even though these first trips may be near your children, know that this pull you feel towards them will dissipate as you learn to live in this new space more.

Due to so many people sharing with me their aches and pains of their children leaving the nest, I wanted to share the fun and excitement that can come from celebrating what awesome parents we've been. Rather than dwell on the negative thoughts, I wanted to help others change their mindset to appreciate all their hard work as a parent and to just let loose and be themselves again.

I'm honored that you're reading this. If it helps, please share with other friends who are struggling with this part of their journey. I hope these fifty chapters help turn your frown upside down. I'm wishing you many quiet moments with a smile on your face as you realize your self-worth and reward yourself for a job well done!

PART ONE

Letting Go – Be Kind to You

1

Their Freshman Semester

For one last time, you gave your child the biggest hug as you said one more goodbye. Pulling away, you made sure to show them a big smile, even though your heart was breaking.

Am I really in this stage of life where I'm saying goodbye to my child as they walk off to their dorm on their own? Holy cow, where did the time go?

There's a change in the air. It feels similar to a magic trick where a magician makes one suddenly disappear. Like our seasons, this new feeling emulates autumn when the trees are letting go of their leaves. At one point everything is green, lush, and normal, but with a blink of an eye, things we see, feel, and hear suddenly change to something totally new.

When we find ourselves as parents in this time of our lives, we need to realize that we have one moment to react correctly in a positive fashion. With our tears held in the back of our mind until the next shower or the drive home alone in the car, our focus needs to create a solid stance showing how reliable and dependable we still are as our college student enters this new phase alone.

Because they are experiencing living somewhat on their own, we need to step up and become a sort of cheerleader for them. If they are playing a sport for their college, we need to show our sincerity as well as cheer them from the sidelines. If they are in clubs instead, we need to show up with our bona fide questions in a stable manner and show our interest in their interests. We need to check in on them like we did for their club and high school sport activities and show our support for them, yet also give them autonomy as well.

Now, with our new technology, colleges stream their games and sports. It is a great feeling to watch them play and then follow up with a call or FaceTime to discuss the outcome. It's quite easy to visit Best Buy and find the needed cables to connect with a laptop or ask how to use wireless methods as well.

By streaming it onto our flat screen TV, it was just as if we were in the stands. During our talks after the volleyball matches, we made sure to stick to the script and ask questions just like during her months of club play at home such as, "How was your warm up?" "How are your knee and ankle braces holding up?" Keep the conversation the same as usual. It helps them feel secure in that familiar tone.

In order to move through the homesick phase in a calm manner, we would remind them to visit friends and family while they were on the other coast. As autumn showed up on the trees, we'd offer ideas such as going to pumpkin patches and apple picking with new friends. If they are within driving distance, a reminder that home is just a few hours away can ease the heartache they might not want to admit to. Although, since our girls were on the other coast, we would send them a favorite sweatshirt from home and candy or snacks in a package sealed with our love.

Since it is their dream of attending their college of choice, it's important to show your approval and support. By sending a Snapchat picture, they'll most likely reciprocate with one back. Now you know where they are and what they're doing Sending a text here and there helps them feel love from home without being overwhelmed. Adding shots of their favorite pet left behind is always sure to put a smile on their faces.

If we think back, leaving home and moving on to the next phase of life is hard. Feeling secure and safe is important for your new college kid. Be part of the transition by offering your devotion. They will experience some kind of homesickness, so be sure to support them and share your homesick stories during this once in a lifetime change. Be available, show calmness, and remember it's their dream.

2

Your Freshman Semester

"There are two things we give our children; one is roots and the other is wings." ~ Johann Wolfgang von Goethe

If we think back to the first time we held those bundles of joy, we can probably recall the hopes and dreams we had for their journey. We wanted them to be the best versions of themselves. As we taught our children well, we aspired to the fact that the rules of our home would help shape them into the responsible independent individuals we always wished for. We hoped to be the parents who showed the best support, so that they would reach any star possible.

In any parenting book out there, no one mentions how much pain comes with this time in our lives when our children leave the nest to live on their own or for college. The most important thing to do in this parenting stage is be kind to yourself.

This stage not only breaks your heart, but can bring negative feelings into this phase. Feelings you've never felt will come spilling out and your tears will feel like they'll never end. Your surroundings will look different and you may feel stuck.

Instead of stuck, remind yourself that you're just sitting in your feelings. In order to free yourself from the pain, you must feel and see the changes, acknowledge them and then accept them.

As you acknowledge them, you are basically surrendering to them. Surrender is a good thing. It helps to release the pain. Releasing and not pushing them down into your body is key.

By crying and feeling your angst, you are allowing your body to release what no longer serves you. Begin to replace the pain with positive ideas such as celebrating this moment. Be your own cheerleader by using positive thoughts and writing about this new place in your journal. Restore your sadness with encouraging thoughts and meditations.

As my first daughter ventured off back East to PA to begin her journey in archaeology, I felt lost. I did notice that as I released my tears on my drive home from work, it opened up a new space. I realized it was up to me to replace this space with ideas that would help me.

I began to help others who were getting ready to enter this mysterious place and hearing myself speak out loud, it helped to comfort me. There was a co-worker who had a daughter who was a senior in high school. She began feeling the same way I did. It was a comfort to help someone else and learn others could benefit from my experience.

By sharing my story with my colleague of how we all traveled to PA to take my oldest to college and all the feelings that came with that experience, she was able to realize what one goes through and she was able to start working on how to help herself now.

As I helped others by sharing my experience, I sought out others that have gone before me. I asked what ideas helped them through the pain. I made sure to practice looking at all new possibilities that lingered in this space and not rush through too quickly.

By sitting in the space of sadness, it helped by letting the feelings surface so that I could release them. I made sure to monitor my alcohol and food intake. I wanted to stay healthy in this crazy place and not just stuff everything down and cover them up with food and alcohol. By holding these sad feelings down, we are actually holding onto the pain and not releasing it.

Be kind. Treat your body and mind like royalty as you enter this change. You deserve this pampering and it will keep you physically healthy and mentally happy. Cheer for yourself, practice releasing your pain, be helpful to others entering the same space, and breathe. As you sit in this new environment, celebrate the fact that you had a big hand in your bundle of joy now living her dream.

3

Enjoy the Missing Clutter

Parenting teenagers is learning how to live in clutter. You had years of living in these disorderly heaps and the good news is you can finally learn to live clutter-free. No more do you have to subject your mind to the overwhelming piles of mess everywhere. By decluttering, you will open up not only your living areas by moving about freely, but you will live with a clearer mind. Now you have an open area to start enjoying your new stage in life.

Now that your college student has taken some of this jumble with them, you can begin to enjoy your living room and do some actual living. You may even have children who finally moved out into their own apartment. Your nest is finally yours again. How many times did you say, "Hey, if you're going upstairs, could you take your things with you?" "How about taking your belongings to your room so others can use the space in the bathroom?" Enjoy using less words and not having to manage others in order to save you trips up the stairs delivering their mess.

Putting yourself first may be a new idea for you, so get excited and start thinking about the things you always wanted to do. This is probably one of the best benefits of becoming an empty nester. You put yourself first. Remember, this is not being selfish. It is a healthy way of loving yourself.

For instance, every time you sat down when your college student was a teenager, you probably found yourself bouncing back up to help them find something, cook something, or take them somewhere. Now, you enter the living room to live how you want. Start a list of all those things you wanted to do, but never got around to. The list might include: organizing old family video tapes, pulling out movies you want to watch, and looking through the pile of magazines purchased, but never viewed.

I remember entering the bathroom after turning off my alarm one morning to start my day. As I turned on the lights and started the shower, I noticed there wasn't an enormous pile of clothes from my daughters. No used towels and dirty clothes on the floor. I actually caught myself smiling in the mirror. I had room to put my own clean towels on the sink counter. I wasn't performing the chore of putting everyone else's belongings away before trying to enjoy a warm shower. Saving time to use on myself was unheard of, but definitely something I could get accustomed to.

Another time that put a smile on my face was entering my home after work. I headed to the couch, flipped my shoes off, and took a big breath. I reached for a magazine and started turning the pages. It was a strange feeling, because it was so quiet. As I looked around I noticed less clutter. It helped me to stay in that space and enjoy my articles. Because I had no time in the past to look through these magazines the way I wanted, I had that kid-at-Christmas feeling. Putting my feet up and letting them feel like they were at a spa in Epsom salts, it was the best treat. What a delight I found by doing two simple things: relaxing my feet and enjoying quiet reading.

There are many things that are bad for our health and environment which in turn has an equal effect on our minds. By using your home areas to your satisfaction, you're helping to create a positive environment in which to dwell stress free.

Finally, you're finding yourself using your bathroom in the manner in which it should be. It's almost like staying at a hotel. Now that your child's daily clutter of books and clothes are nowhere to be found in your living room, enjoy your mind feeling more focused. You are now enjoying different rooms of your home that you pay good money for every month. This will allow you to sit more comfortably in those moments when you're missing them. Furthermore, these newly cleaned rooms will keep a smile on your face.

4

Admire the Clean Kitchen Sink

"Hooray! It's a miracle! I can see the bottom of the sink and it's clean!" I shouted one day living as an empty nester. After all those years of coming home from work and seeing stacks of dishes, it is a thrill to experience no dishes in the sink.

Thinking back to all the carpooling and driving to a second job, I don't miss coming home to that horrible sight of dishes stacked to the heavens. Finally seeing the bottom of your sink is as if you're looking at a fresh new one. Although you miss your college student, you might be thinking how great this empty nest just might be?

Now that you're in charge, you can fill it up as much as you want and you get to keep it as clean as you want to your heart's content. It may, however, bring up your feelings of missing them too. But allow yourself to feel those feelings and then let them go.

Mothers are accustomed to stepping into a teen's room to grab dirty laundry and gather the dirty dishes. Because it was part of our daily ritual, moms are in a habit of stopping by and collecting the bowls and cups teetering on every ledge.

As we notice the emptiness of their room and no dirty dishes in sight, we're relieved at first that we don't have to bus their room like a waitress. Nevertheless, this is where your heart will start beating faster. Since they're no longer there, there's nothing to pick up after. It does bring some sense of relief, although a mother's heart will show up right at this moment.

In comes that wave of pain of missing them, just as we thought we had it under control and all cried out. Remember that this is normal and it definitely doesn't mean you're losing your mind. You're just a mom who misses your child.

As the feelings start to surface and your tears begin to well up, simply let them out. This is a great time to remind yourself that it's fine and give yourself permission to let your feelings out. Believe me, when you let your emotions out, it's a great time to practice feeling and letting go of what no longer serves you.

When I practiced the habit of walking into their room hunting down any soiled dishware, my feelings would stop me in my tracks. I recall thinking, "I can let these emotions out now or later, but they need to be felt in order to leave." So I've found myself hanging out in their room sometimes.

While I walked into their room, I felt those feelings come up. I'd find myself lying on their bed and looking around. I remember thinking, "Wow, this was their perspective from this side." Experiencing what their view was all those years ago from their bed was pretty neat. I looked around their room seeing their posters and special photos they had hanging on their walls.

Because we were still in the same home when they were infants, it made me think back to where the rocking chair was and all those moments holding them thinking, "I wonder what's in store for them when they get older?" It's a strange feeling going in and out of those moments, but also very rewarding.

If times like this bring up sadness and a tearful moment, don't hesitate to let them emerge. Remind yourself it's a normal feeling and part of the steps of watching them leave the nest. They may only fester within if you keep them inside. Holding onto them may only ignite other problems such as drinking and overeating to cover and hide the pain. In this sense, let yourself off the hook and pardon these feelings.

Obviously, when you start feeling less sadness as you walk in and out of their room, you know you're on your way. Heck, now you have another space to enjoy in your home. Now that you're in a good place, enjoy that empty sink and the beginnings of your graduation into your empty nest.

5

Let Your Emotions Out

As you said goodbye to your college student, it triggered many emotions such as fear, sorrow, and joy all at the same time. Now that these feelings have presented themselves, you may be recognizing them at a higher level than normal which is becoming worrisome.

If you ask me, giving birth to them is as emotional as saying goodbye to them. Emotions are very delicate and extremely hard to control at times. Since emotions come from our willingness and our perception along with judgment of a reaction to something, they come along with physiological changes in our body. It is very important to notice these changes that are unusual and unique to us. Huge changes in our lives or our way of life can trigger these feelings making us notice that we are crying, shaking, and even perspiring more than normal.

It may take time to sort through them, but we must be

aware that these are normal outcomes as we venture through the empty nester stage. As we notice these changes, we need to help create a calm space by understanding that this is a normal part of life.

While having any big changes in our lives, our emotions will use alarms such as these feelings to warn our brains. When we realize that we all experience these moments and feelings to extreme levels, it can help us to move back on track. Clearly, it's time to give ourselves permission to move through this stage slowly. There's no need to rush. By learning new strategies, we can become prepared which is the best medicine for our anxious heart.

Since our culture sees sadness and crying as a weakness, we may fall back into those past beliefs that we had growing up. Many of us grew up in the family motto that crying is for babies. We've been told "don't cry", "there's nothing to cry about", "grow up", and "suck it up".

Researchers have uncovered that the best way to heal from these emotions is to lean into them and not numb them. They also say the more you struggle to ignore these feelings, they only invite more of the same. Once we learn new coping strategies in this new stage of life, we realize that this is the process of life and everyone goes through the same emotions. The secret is how we handle ourselves through it.

By numbing the feeling of these intense emotions with alcohol or drugs or by trying to control eating habits of eating too much or too little, we are only avoiding the pain and trying to escape. That's our body's protective concept of fight or flight. Some try to escape by checking out of life. My family of origin was the model of that concept.

My parents decided not to experience their happiness and instead shut it off to their children. Because they were in deep seclusion from their own childhood feelings, as adults they never dealt with their emotions by learning how to deal with them. Instead, they never showed love verbally or physically by saying "I love you" or hugging. When we went on vacation, it was only our father who took us. Although not divorced, this separate way of living under the same roof showed us all how they were numbing themselves from feeling any emotions. Having to live in a world where you noticed loving examples in other families, but not your own, was very conflicting for us as children.

By not living in joy or happiness, it was a feeling of being stuck. Once I was gone from home for a few years and returned, it was very apparent. It made me weep for my childhood because I felt like I was cheated out of love.

As our family lived in this environment of our parents ignoring the discrepancy of happiness in our household, we learned how to live in a quiet surrounding feeling afraid to speak out about our own feelings. This not only taught us to stuff our emotions and not see their importance in our lives, but created so much exhaustion.

If I think back, they were always exhausted from avoiding their feelings and running away from them. This was seen in the fake ways that they acted; one moment they were acting in a loving way by holding hands in public, but the next moment they were never seen sitting on the couch together to simply watch a television show.

The best gift you can give yourself is to let your emotions out. Simply breathing relieves stress built up in your body, telling yourself this is normal and that you're going to be ok. Also, viewing on your phone a picture from a past vacation with your kids along with the other ideas are great daily coping skills.

Learn and practice these coping strategies in order to live through life's daily moments. Most importantly, remember to create time to check in with yourself three times a day by simply setting alarms and dealing with the feelings that have surfaced.

Finding a support group and creating a balance in your life between work and play can help you cope with your emotions. Be sure to seek professional help if the emotions begin to alter your work and home activities. If you are having unusual back pain, headaches, constipation, or even an upset stomach when you have these feelings, it's important to seek medical advice and be truthful. By hearing your symptoms, they may be able to direct you to an answer. It may not be a pill needed for the cure, but sessions with a professional therapist to help you learn your coping strategies.

Emotions can alter your life if you let them take complete control. These tears are tears of joy because you have successfully accomplished what your end goal was: raising responsible and independent adults.

In my experience, some of the examples you hear may seem too simple and you may even become judgmental with yourself thinking you should have thought of these on your own. Above all, give yourself a break and find the balance that will help you get back on track, and get ready to see your college student at their parents' weekend or next holiday.

6

Take One Day at a Time

It's funny how we use our time to dwell in the past and stay in negativity sometimes. We know it's better to be positive, yet we make our bodies suffer by putting them through these past memories. It may be the past security blanket feeling we're trying to recreate.

If we focus on our children being gone until Thanksgiving or longer, our sadness starts to take over. What we need to be doing is step into living right now, in the present by not looking backwards or forwards. Having a healthy mind can be as easy as putting more focus on the present which in turn lowers our stress level and helps us by getting back to enjoying every day.

Taking action right away is fundamental for success here. It's like jumping rope; you have to just see an opportunity and go for it. One way to get into this positive place and live one day at a time is starting with easy short methods that you can build on. Simply doing breathing exercises every day is a great start. By simply setting your phone to remind you to take a 5 minute breathing break three times a day will help immensely. Give yourself permission to take these short breaks throughout the day. The breathing will not only help your stress level, but will help you start to clear your mind.

In addition to these breaks, schedule 5 minutes of your lunch to meditate. Listen to a meditation in a quiet space at work or venture out to your car for more privacy. After each meditation session, reward yourself with something easy you like to do after work. Use your alarm to find time to start writing in a gratitude journal every day. As you start putting your mind on these daily practices, you will start to feel lighter and you'll begin to use each minute of the day to your advantage.

Studies show that deep breathing strengthens your brain and boosts attention span, small rewards help us use dopamine as a motivator, and being grateful can literally change our brain. Through this important link between our breath and brain, having a focused breath can help our bodies function in other ways. Not only does breathing help with focus, but it helps other bodily functions as well.

As you breathe more and create more noradrenaline for your brain, in return the brain and lungs can communicate better with each other. Too much can wreak havoc on our gastrointestinal motility when those stressing are breathing too much. Since humans have an innate awareness of their environments and what they need to survive, it is important for our security, comfort, and familiarity that our surroundings be positive. Retailers and hospitality industries already know this and make sure that these qualities are present in the music and decor in their establishments.

In regards to using your surroundings as a motivator, plan rewards that take you into a favorable environment that you enjoy. The origins of motivation come from neuroscience. However, here's the quick lowdown on Dopamine for Dummies. In the article, Your Brain on Dopamine: The Science of Motivation by Kevan Lee, he talks about how neurotransmitters are the ones that carry chemical messages that play out in your brain. He tells us that one of these neurotransmitters is dopamine and how its chemical signal gets passed from one neuron to the other.

Without getting into all the jobs of the neurons and receptors in the brain, dopamine is what flows when we anticipate that something good, or a reward, is about to occur. Research shows that dopamine can spike when we prepare for a good reward, consequently we become motivated to receive the reward. Once we practice coming up with these little rewards for living more in the present instead of the past, these spikes of dopamine can act like motivators.

We can use these to help us move forward and to live each moment at a time. In regards to using gratitude to change the brain, Researchers at Trinity College Institute of Neuroscience and the Global Brain Health Institute found that when we focus too much on our problems we stress. We actually create too much noradrenaline which in turn wreaks havoc on our focus, heart rate, and blood pressure.

According to UCLA's Mindfulness Awareness Research Center, frequently articulating gratitude, the quality of being thankful and readiness to show appreciation, literally changes the molecular structure of the brain. It keeps the gray matter functioning, and makes us healthier and happier. Some find that writing in a journal on a daily basis can lead to a happy smile. Practicing grateful writing helps those of us stressed out as well as those with mental health issues or concerns. It gets out your toxic emotions whether shared or not.

In respect to using my own dopamine to motivate myself, I celebrate living in the present by having a coffee with a friend, walking on the beach or in the neighborhood, and going for a bike ride. Since these are the fun things I love, as I use them in my day, I actually increase my dopamine which in turn increases my happiness.

These small changes in my environment keep me living in the present and stop the constant thoughts of missing my college kids. Along with all these outings, I found that writing down at least a few things I'm grateful for each day helps me let go of the stress. By focusing on all the good I possess, it allows me to let go of the stress.

By simply incorporating breathing, enjoying small rewards that are fun,, and writing down things of gratitude, you can help yourself move from a sad person living in the past mindset to one who walks around with a smile on their face while keeping their brain healthy.

Whatever issues you're working on, keep in mind that we can't change the past, but we can change how we view each day with healthy thoughts. These ideas help us stay happy and healthy by not wishing away the days until our college kids come home. By pulling over to see the beauty in your surroundings, you will increase your dopamine and benefit from taking one day at a time.

7

Enjoy the Quiet – The Learned Point of the Soul

Serenity and quiet are two words that truly give description as they are being spoken. That being said, where do you find yours?

In the last chapter, we touched on how significant quiet can be for our stress. In addition, this chapter will go further to show exact ways to include quiet moments daily, how to ease meditation into your daily planner, and how to deal with the fears and baggage that show up in these quiet times.

Once we hear that fears and old baggage show up during this quiet time, we might want to do anything we can to avoid those negative aspects. No one looks forward to fears or the old thoughts from their past to haunt them; however this chapter will show specific ways of working through them in order to help them release.

These thoughts bring up fears in us because they come with feelings such as abandonment, being ignored, not heard, and living in a state of no joy or happiness. Because our parents had their own baggage, they might have ignored us, withheld love and not offered physical hugs, and called us negative names while trying to cope with our daily lives of homework, school problems, and chores. We no longer have to live in that past or any past.

Luckily, there are simple to follow steps to help squash these fears. Starting these easy steps can take us to our paths toward joy. By using our phones, we can conveniently set up three different times during our day to take breathing breaks. As these alarms go off, we need to act upon them. Inside our notes app, we can have an affirmation ready at hand to repeat to create a positive atmosphere and a picture of our family at our favorite place.

By breathing and creating this space in the present, we are allowing the quiet to enter our mind. In order to get these daily breaks to stick, we need to use the old adage of consistency. By doing something for twenty one days, it begins to form as a habit and becomes easier to do. We start looking forward to positive new routines.

Nonetheless, when we hear the word meditation, we may feel uncomfortable because it is foreign to us. A simple beginning point is to turn on soothing music in a quiet area with headphones and sit and just listen. This can take place in the morning and at lunch break with eyes opened or closed. The more pleasant this is, the more you will do it.

Let any thoughts come to mind and put your main attention on having a clear mind as you meditate your way. As you listen to soothing music at home for your third time of the day, let it be a notification to your mind that you are ready to have negative thoughts from the past come up. Since you have a clearer mind from your practice, this allows for your stuffed baggage to appear and to be released.

The only job you have is easy; simply let any old thoughts connected to unfavorable feelings surface. There is no need to relive them, only see them for what they were, look for a lesson you can learn, and thank the thoughts for showing up to teach you.

If you feel tears well up, you know you're on the right track. It may be a thought from your past that triggers the emotion. While meditating and letting your feelings bubble up, you may question and wonder why you never did something in the past. For me, mine was not finishing some school projects. When I let the thought come full view, I remember that I never completed my projects at school that I needed help with. Because my father was so intelligent, he didn't like it if I asked questions, so I never got the help I needed or asked for.

I always felt that I was supposed to know the answer to everything. The feelings of inadequacy and not being enough were the ones that showed up. By letting these feelings come up, I could see the real reason why I wasn't given help. It wasn't my fault, rather my father's Aspergers and perfectionism coming out. As you let your emotions release, you will feel more happiness and joy.

Your tears may fall and that is normal. You will notice these ah-ha moments and reasons why things happened. It will show that your hurt comes from someone else's pain. As these bubble up and have a chance to be observed, they will slip away. That is how things are let go.

It's not that we let them go, they let go of us. As you practice sitting in this quiet space, you will find yourself looking forward to this time. Even though the quiet space might feel uncomfortable and cold at first, remember there is no correct way to meditate. Simply breathe, smile and do it your way.

8

Be Prepared to Hear How Others Want You to Feel

When you step into this stage of being an empty nester, others, whether in the stage or not, will have their opinion on how you're going to feel.

Those who haven't entered this stage will try to use their statements that helped them so far. However since they aren't even in this stage, they don't know what they're talking about. On the other hand, those who are in the empty nest stage now will use confident words because they had to struggle through the sad moments already. Be prepared to hear them tell you how you're supposed to feel.

In the long run, if you use the concept of treating everyone with love, you'll come out of this with flying colors. We have to remember that most people mean well, but they don't always have the nicest words to show it.

Because they have felt the pain when they first entered this stage, they are living from the other side. They forget the sadness and the adjustments that had to be made to get where they are now. By remembering that others are only trying to help, take each statement with a grain of salt and be sure to offer a smile for their helpful words.

When others offer their words of thought, they think they are actually being helpful. In a way, they are trying to use their kindness, but don't realize that others have to go through the stage of an empty nest on their own. By announcing their opinion before being asked, they don't realize that they are hurting more than helping. Because some people don't ever show or deal with their own feelings, they make others feel a lack of strength by dismissing your feelings.

"Yes, your children are gone, but you'll be fine. No need to be sad." Right there is someone putting their journey of their emotions onto yours. Stay in the fact that you are aware of the feelings you'll have and tell yourself these people are most likely acting out of love, but lack the personal experience of being an empty nester..

As you meet up with friends who are already empty nesters, they'll ask how you're feeling but then change it to "this is how you should feel" conversation. Because we are fresh in this stage, we still have the feelings of sadness from missing them and not seeing them in the house anymore. Be prepared to hear how easy it is to get through and how it won't even hurt a bit. Those words right there are lies. It isn't easy, it will hurt, and it might feel like a lot. All I heard was, "You'll be fine. Don't worry, everyone goes through it."

The best way to avoid being wrapped up in someone else's false sayings is to politely exit the conversation. By staying in their conversation, all you'll hear are the problems and feelings they still have, but are masking.

Besides those who already entered this stage, there are those who have school aged children still living in their home. They are still on the sports journey with them and try to offer you how easy it will be to let them go. Since these parents are living in an overwhelmed state, they can't imagine your stage or pain and throw out the generic, "It's fine and you'll be fine." Again, these people mean well by trying to show their kindness and help; however they're not in the right place to tell you how to feel.

While in this stage, it is the best opportunity to deal with your feelings. Sometimes it actually brings in feelings of abandonment that you may have felt as a child, but never dealt with all these years. Give yourself permission to feel anyway you want.

The secret is as you let these feelings come up, that's a sign that they're ready to be seen and released. By not stuffing these feelings down, or pushing them aside, you will master how you're supposed to feel. How lucky for the friends that enter this stage after you. Now they have someone who won't just regurgitate that everything is fine, but who can be there for them cheering them on.

9

Let Them Be Who They Are

It is different learning the process of letting things go vs. letting go of ideas because we can't just let go of certain emotions; they let go of us when they've healed. Keep this in mind as you venture through this section of Letting Go.

Now that you've lived through your goodbyes and are in your newly quiet nest, it's important to let your college student be who they are and let them live on their own. We can't very well learn letting go if we know every aspect they are involved in if we are constantly trying to maneuver their actions like puppet strings through constant calls and texts. Consequently, this is the perfect time to learn strategies for this and be kind to yourself all at the same time.

If you were the mom who made many calls and texts when your child was in high school, it's time to practice ways of putting a limit on them. College is the phase in life where they learn how to do things on their own. This period is where they use what they've learned or had modeled to them and start making decisions on their own.

When it comes to pulling back on the calls and texts, there are some rules you can make with fun cheats you can do to be kind to your heart during this sensitive time. Use technology like Snapchat, Instagram or Facebook to see what they're doing without being the "helicopter mom". Be sure to have a rule such as "must reply something" when receiving texts from either parent. By inserting a new rule of replying, it decreases worry for parents and keeps your students hassle free.

By using different social media, you can wean yourself from the previous large amount of texting and calling. First, use Snapchat in a nonchalant way that will be soothing and fun for your heart. With Snapchat, I take a picture of where I am. (These pictures only last a few seconds when sent.) Next, I'll add a filter by swiping or typing a short message. Maybe I'm at a fast food joint or see their favorite cookies at the grocery store as I shop. I take the picture, type a quick 3-4 word message, and then hit send. In return, they'll most likely return a Snapchat where they are at that moment.

When I missed them, I did this only a few times a day. I would immediately see that they were getting ready for volleyball or swim practice, hanging in their dorm room, or at the library. Because the photos sent on Snapchat are in real time, they help you see exactly where they are at that moment. It is a great way to calm your heart and know your chick-a-dee is fine.

Because of the "must reply" rule, you may receive a text telling you they are busy. Even when I would make a call aware of their schedule, I would receive texts telling me they were in class or working in a group project. Instead of being bummed because you don't get to hear their voice, be happy in the fact that you know where they are, and they're safe and sound. I always sent a thumbs-up or said thanks with a heart. They seemed to appreciate it.

As a hands-on-mom from the past, it will be hard implementing these strategies to curtail your calls and texts, however in the long run you will be grateful. By not hounding your college student with never ending calls and texts, you are allowing them to mature and grow into that responsible person you wanted. In the long run, by backing off with calls and texts, it gives them the opportunity to miss you and text or call you.

Having to go from being a hands-on-mom hearing from them daily, to only minimal calls and texts is hard on a mom's heart and emotions. As a parent, remind yourself that this special beginning time where your child leaves home is another learning experience for them. Equally, it is important that we limit our communication in order for our child to grow into a responsible person and promote independence.

10

Help Them Take on Their Own Responsibilities

Responsible means that one is accountable for their own decisions, controls, and management of their everyday lives.

As a mom, we did so many things for them, but little by little we lifted some of our control to let them take the reins. We didn't necessarily lift all control especially in the areas of their school assignments and making health appointments. However, this is the perfect time to hand them all the reins with us in support mode only.

One of the hardest things to do is say no to our child. But when it comes to them asking us to help coordinate their assignments' due dates, it's definitely time to step back. Even though we are concerned about their health and wellness, it is important for them to pick up the phone to make their own doctor and dentist appointments. It is time to remind them they are in adulthood and it's their turn to do so. As they use their sweet talk and charm on your motherly heart, be sure to keep in mind that they need to be the one to do these things for themselves. By staying true to you, here are some strategies that work.

Cutting your help out all together is neither necessary nor feasible. However, it is time for them to stand on their own. When their professor hands out the syllabus, it's their turn to take charge of their learning. The same goes for them making a doctor appointment when feeling ill. Since they are at school, it is important for them to track down the health office on campus and get help. In this new phase of their lives, you become more of a liaison where you can offer steps on how to speak to a professor or what to say when making a doctor appointment. By continuing to be a connection for them, you are helping them transition into adulthood.

It's time for helicopter moms to land and enjoy life. Sorry to say, but professors don't and won't communicate with parents about the student's assignments. It's time to promote independence and let them take their personality out for a spin.

If they are accustomed to your steady involvement, it's time to let them solve their own problems. This is not to say you cut all ties. If they ask for help on an assignment, turn the questions toward them by asking, "What avenues can you take to complete the assignment?" If they are completely lost, remind them to speak with a classmate. They can simply treat this new friend out to the college café for a little treat with coffee and bounce some ideas off them. Remind them that each professor has office hours where students make appointments to discuss their need for help on any assignment. Let them know that colleges are communities where they can seek help for anything.

When it comes to scheduling doctor and dentist appointments for them, my advice is DON'T. Since they never had to do it on their own, it will make them feel uncomfortable but that is where the secret to growth lies. In a kind way, tell them you won't be doing this anymore, but offer phrases and questions they can ask. Walk them through what they can expect. This will help them become an individual who can take care of themselves.

When our volleyball player hurt her knee, it was up to her to not only reschedule future appointments, but to arrange for transportation to and from the office. Since the doctor's office goes through the student with insurance questions, she would relay them to her father. These discussions helped her understand the questions and what to reply. By helping them through this area, they will be able to ask questions of their own health care provider when that time comes.

Letting go of habits is hard to do. Remind yourself that only good will come from their uncomfortable feelings during this change. It will take practice, tears, and time, so don't give up. By moving through each day, it will get easier and you will see the plan of letting go start to work.

As you practice, these sad feelings will begin to let go of you as you replace them with this new viable approach. Not only will you be changing things for the good of your relationship, but you will let them be who they truly are. The more they live in the feeling of discomfort, the more growth will occur. As a result, through this independent time, they are learning important social skills that will help them prosper in their adulthood.

11

Allow Others to Do Things Their Way

With Letting Go as the theme, it is important to be kind to yourself and your partner. You've been doing things your way for many years and you have your own groove doing them. However, it's not only you. You may notice your spouse will do things around the house differently than you.

Come to think about it, some of the things they do are driving you crazy. Since you're so accustomed to doing things your way, how are you going to let this go? Three things you can do are breathe, observe their way, and use kind words when communicating.

Once our girls went off to college, it was up to my husband and I to clean: dishes, bathrooms, and overall vacuuming. Most of these chores were done by the girls and me when they were home. Because I had a system of my own, it would bother me to watch him do the various cleaning. He seemed to be cleaning in ways opposite of me. I had to breathe after observing his ways and remind myself that change is here to help me use kindness in my communication.

For instance, he would fill up one side of the sink and soak the pots and pans with utensils overnight. I, on the other hand, would soak for only 10-15 minutes and then finish washing them before bed. Sometimes when left overnight, it would hog the use of the sink while I would be trying to make breakfast and coffee the next morning.

By breathing, I reminded myself that it really isn't the end of the world. When I observed how he attacked cleaning projects, I learned that when he soaked them, he was actually using less water and making them easier to clean. His way used less resources and less elbow grease. Once I decided to chat with him, I could tell him in a kind way how it slowed me down in the morning if soaking was left too long. In addition, I could let him know the helpful things I learned from his ways of cleaning.

Sometimes we have a way of cleaning that requires a certain amount of time. It takes time so that areas get clean to avoid illness. If the shower, toilets, and sinks aren't being cleaned for a certain amount of time in order to kill bacteria and viruses, we can end up getting sick or pass it onto others

My husband would rush through these areas when cleaning. It was important for me to breathe and while observing his way of cleaning, point out the good things before telling him the importance of taking time for a thorough clean. Again, it is important to use kind words because who wants to be lectured when they are doing something their way? In order for others to see our logic, we have to give them time to soak it up to have complete understanding.

Since this is a new stage in our lives, it is a great time to evaluate your personal growth. One goal in life is to learn and better ourselves by showing love to others. By using the three points of breathing, observing, and communicating with kind words, what better way to learn new ways of doing things.

We're like a good merlot. As we age, we only get better. By coming out of our usual routine, we can see how taking a breath and observing our own ways can relax us and help push us up to another level of being. You are allowing what no longer serves you to be released and let it know it's time to Let Go. As you examine more of your actions, suddenly you'll see your new level change for the good.

12

Remind Yourself This Isn't Forever

When we move into this new stage of our life, it comes with a feeling of uncertainty. This in turn brings on an uncomfortable feeling and may cause panic in some. Your mind may trick you to think it will last forever. I recall my mind constantly replaying my thought that this was the end of the road with my kids. As you get caught up in these emotions, turn to the things that you know are true and all the aspects that helped you in life before.

Feeling like something will last forever is having a sad emotion so deep that you don't see it ending. When you look back at all the stages of your child, see all the successes that were built. We made it through all the firsts where we thought there was no end in sight for our sadness. In the end, we realized we were part of those achievements, so now we can treat this new stage like any other time before. With that knowledge, it's time to put our smile back on our faces.

One such stage was dealing with the feedings every two hours. As I think back, I can remember thinking that this will never end and I just might go insane. Hearing them cry before and after feedings always made me think, "Is this going to be forever?" Struggling through feedings every two hours makes every mom think it will never end. However, as we think back to those moments, we recognize we came out of the other side of forever. If we are honest with ourselves, we felt the "forever" feeling quite often through their growing stages and made it through them all happily.

Another stage was taking them to kindergarten for the first time. By doing this, it changed everything. If we stayed home with them up to this point, we had to release them into the real world. We didn't have control and that was a scary place. We had to deal with that feeling of forever. Even if we were dropping them off, it was different from daycare.

Now that they are off to college, you can relate to your past feelings of forever. Let yourself off the hook knowing that this is okay. I can tell you that it was sad and hard at times, but as you think back to all the stages that you moved through, your sadness transforms into happiness. By using aspects that helped you in the past, you will be out of this stuck feeling in no time. If you think back, you made it through those emotions and you'll do the same here.

As a result, you used your strength as well as knowing that it wasn't forever. This stage will bring old feelings of dismay, but it comes with wonderful qualities. You can see your success in raising this child to an adult which comes with your graduation from the feeling of "forever". By giving yourself time, just like you did in the past, you will see yourself unstuck from that emotion of forever and moving on.

13

How to Maneuver through the Holidays

When the holidays come round, we start feeling the excitement in the air. If our grown child is returning home for this festive time, we begin our lists for the grocery store, our Christmas present list, and a schedule of all the forced-family-fun we have in mind. Before you put pen to paper, take a breath, remind yourself they are grown, and things are going to be different. However, here come some amazing ideas to help you through this new time to have a memorable visit.

With change, our minds will take our heart on a rollercoaster of frustration and disappointment, or we can prepare our hearts during this change by eliminating expectations. Our intentions come from our past celebrations. We may think back to all the different activities and traditions we did when our children were younger. Because sometimes we still see them that way, we have a strong belief that they will want to do all the same things we've always done when they were younger.

Since our grown children have been living on their own for a few years now, we need to reel in our expectations and see them at their age now. Because they haven't lived within our family schedule, we must realize that they have been doing things on their time schedule and will most likely have some plans of their own. They may have a new girlfriend or college friends who live nearby, plans to go away with others, or they may have different feelings about the good 'ol family traditions.

While your grown child has been fending for herself in the adult world on her own, it is up to us to connect and ask questions that will help all hearts and minds stay grounded, happy, and living in truth. Before they venture home for the holidays, find time to ask them what they want to do during their stay. Because I'm aware of some of their likes, I made sure to ask one daughter if she wanted to bake cookies and which kind.

For years she has enjoyed baking cookies for our local firemen who work on Christmas Eve and Christmas Day away from their families. I would be sure to have those ingredients ready for her. I would ask both daughters if they were interested in attending a Christmas Eve service, if they wanted our traditional Christmas Eve dinner of salmon and asparagus, and if there were any new traditions they wanted to do. Since they returned home on different days, I let them select a favorite place to have lunch after getting picked up from the airport. I also made sure to ask them if they want to visit any nearby zoos or museums.

If you are unsure how to word some questions, here are some to try. You can simply say, "Hey, I'm trying to get a grocery list started for your stay. Is there anything special I can pick up for you? Are you interested in our traditional family dinner or do you have other plans? As the dates get closer, are there any activities you want to do with us so we can take time off from work?"

By asking questions similar to these, you're communicating to them as adults and finding out if they plan on being home on Christmas Eve as well as finding out what plans and expectations they've had floating around in their heads about their stay.

Furthermore when asking these questions ahead of time, you are offering a friendly opening for them and saving your heart from disappointment. This, in turn, creates a loving path for everyone to speak and share their ideas. By providing this positive space, it will keep fighting and disagreements at bay. This will also give you time to live with their plans when they don't jive with yours. It gives you time to deal with the feelings that the changes brought up and helps keep the atmosphere positive when they do arrive.

When you practice communicating to them in this manner, it allows you to connect with your grown children with love and not frustrations. It also offers them a new expectation of their parents listening to their needs, and it will be a space they'll be willing to come visit more often. You will experience smiles from them because they will see you are treating them like the grown adult they have become.

PART TWO

Recalling Your Favorites

14

Remember Your Favorite Things & Do Them

As soon as your children head to college, you will notice all the extra free time you have in your life. If you were spending every weekend traveling to a different city for your child's sport, you will definitely notice the available time that exists. Enjoy a few moments just by inhaling and exhaling while being grateful that you survived all those years on the road. Now, what better way to help contribute to your health and wellness than to think back to your favorite things as you practice your breathing techniques and see yourself starting these fun activities again.

Now that we begin to notice a large chunk of time available, we can fill it in two ways: either by putting bad things into our body while watching senseless television programming, or we can think back to the things we enjoyed doing and start those again or even try something entirely new.

Since becoming an empty nester can be stressful and comes with sadness, we have an opportunity to do something that promotes health and happiness. Remembering a former favorite activity or hobby can create less negativity for the mind, make life feel meaningful again and provide physical, mental, and emotional benefits to have a well-rounded life.

Based on research at Kettering University and other psychologists, doing your favorite thing or hobby can show you an alternative to worrying and more importantly help you lead a relaxing and stress free life. It is a great way to move the mind into a place of relaxation. Getting back to exercise such as hiking and biking can help our physical and emotional health.

Research completed by several psychologists of about 1,400 individuals found that their new activity helped lower their blood pressure and total cortisol leading to a smaller waist. Even low movement hobbies, like knitting and crafting, are associated with having better health. As we start filling this vacant time with enjoyable activities, we will feel our heart calm.

Once we noticed that we weren't traveling every weekend both Saturday and Sunday to Los Angeles for our daughter's volleyball tournaments, a feeling of relief came over us. We started by just enjoying being home. Of course, we had many little chores to work on and things to fix, but we also started doing the things that brought a smile to our faces. My husband started surfing more and I began going on more bike rides throughout the neighborhood. With the breeze in my hair and the fresh smell of the flowers, it was very helpful in calming my mind of all my worries.

Another joy we found was doing puzzles and playing card games. A 1,000 piece puzzle puts your mind on your present moment. It really puts worrying on the back burner. Card games were always a favorite pastime, but fell off when their needs came first. Getting back to the friendly competition has been very enjoyable.

One Saturday, we remembered a board game we played when we were younger. Out of nowhere that morning, my husband announced we needed to get dressed because we were going to the store to get that game. Allow yourself to have more spontaneity as you live in this new open area.

As a result, we took pictures and sent them or called the girls when we needed help remembering certain rules. When you're in this fun mode, it's good to see that sitting around worrying isn't useful. Making the best of your time is more beneficial.

Stress brought on by negative thoughts, such as worry, can create a chain reaction in your body. When your brain detects a stressor, you have an increase in cortisol and blood pressure which then causes a sour relationship with your tissues and organs. As this happens you are putting yourself into a "fight or flight" mode as your adrenaline raises your heart rate and oxygen levels in your muscles. This puts extreme harm onto your heart. By adopting fun activities and hobbies back into your world, it creates a happier and healthier you.

Whereas stress can have a great impact on many parts of our body, it's vital to find things to help us calm our minds and stay serene. Focusing on positive aspects of our life is a great step to take. Filling every free moment with positive fun like a game or bike ride is a great start. Now that we have made it through so much with our children and finally have them off to college, it's time for us to do things to keep our hearts healthy. Find the fun and joyful part of yourself again.

15

Reminisce the Fun Times

She came up to me at the age of two while I was doing the dishes. Her little hand holding a half eaten apple was being raised up to my eyesight. As I look at it I hear her say, "Can you make it juicy again?" In a fluster, I took it and thought how the heck am I gonna do that? The cold water was running so I simply put the apple under it, shook off the excess, and handed it back. To my surprise as I was crossing my fingers, she gave it a bite, looked at me with a smile and said, "Thanks Mom!"

Best memory ever! As you recall your favorite ones, you'll have a smile from ear to ear. When we look back at these past experiences, we need to be sure to see how much fun existed and what we actually created. Be sure to skip this idea if you become too upset. If this brings up deep sad emotions and feelings, work on letting them come up so they can be released. This needs to be done as a reminder and not a chore. To reminisce, we need to see the positive aspects in every fun memory.

Because the beginning of the empty nest stage is filled with a lot of feelings of missing your children, the mind and heart live in a state of sadness and confusion for a while as they adjust. In order to help adapt, reminiscing about the enjoyable times spent with your kids from the past can bring a smile to your face and joy in your heart. This is a perfect idea to help move through this new stage.

By focusing on the positivity of the cheerful times from the past, you are definitely helping your heart rate and blood pressure. These moments can also show parents how much fun and excitement they created.

Looking back at old videos and photo albums can help you remember all the fun times. A lot of these might show up as you clean up their rooms or other areas of your home. Because writing a gratitude journal is very healthy for our mind and body, you can start to list these fun times as they come to mind. Simply jotting them down and writing a small memory helps the heart.

As I was going through an area of my entertainment unit, I came across my old videos. Because they are still on VHS tapes, I plopped them in their cartridge adapter and viewed them. Since I took time years ago to share them with my girls when they were about middle school age, I had written down what each tape showed. Valentine's Day was approaching and I selected those that showed them as babies with red balloons and older with all their Valentine notes from classmates along with goodies. Seeing them brought back so many wonderful feelings. It was definitely a cure when I was missing them.

When they came home with their fiancés during the holidays, it was so much fun to watch them flip through the photo albums I had worked on before phone pictures became a big deal. I would take my film to the local bulk store for developing and then chronologically put them in photo albums. Watching them look at them with their future husbands was a real treat. It was awesome to hear their questions about where they were and what they were doing. It was fun seeing them relive and reminisce. My children's expressions were priceless.

In the 1960's, Dr. Robert Butler, a psychiatrist who specialized in geriatric medicine, found that reminiscing could be therapeutic and helpful to put their elder patients' lives in perspective. Although we are still pretty spry, strategies used for the elderly work here for us empty nesters just as well. Reminiscing therapy is also found to be a non-pharmacological intervention that improves self-esteem and provides a sense of fulfillment and comfort.

Certainly as parents, we can look back at all the tremendous times we created to reinvigorate our energies in order to focus on their goals of success in their college work. Not only does reminiscing give us a boost of positivity, but also gives meaning to all the work we've done. When we reminisce, our kids can join in during a phone call or FaceTime session. Along with the memories we tell, these will definitely help us through times in the future when we need a joyful boost.

16

Become a Better Parent

There are many aspects to think about as you look around your empty nest; however this one is probably the most important. Now that your children are out there behaving like adults, it is time to start treating them as such. We all see our children as the small tikes that needed us to hold their hand as they crossed the street. In actuality, they are grown and live on their own at college. While they are away from home, this is the perfect time to step into this next phase.

Over the years, we've seen them become high school seniors attending their prom and then graduation. As they head off to college, parents might take a glimpse through photo albums or look up pictures of their children when they were youngsters.

There isn't anything wrong with this, but parents need to keep their frame of mind on the fact that their child is a grown up. They'll be doing their own laundry, getting their meals, and being in charge of their assignments. This is the picture we need to have in our mind in order to begin to treat them in that fashion.

Having the grown version in our mind is the answer to the solution of being a better parent. If we think about it, we don't baby our friends when we enjoy their company at dinner or just picking up a coffee. That kind of behavior would be unheard of, yet some parents fall into that rut. When we receive a call, we need to ask what they've been doing and make sure we visualize that in our head. By constantly seeing them as an adult in our mind, this will spill over when it comes time to interact with them.

When they come home for a visit after living on their own a bit, of course we're not going to cut their meat for them; how silly that would be! Instead treat them the same way you would any adult visiting, except that you have a life long loving connection with them.

As dinner approaches, there is no reason why you can't ask them to help out to prepare or set up as we might ask any other adult staying for a meal. While asking about their life, be of mind to not jump or try to fix something if they speak of a problem. On the other hand, ask what ways they tried to fix the problem. Keeping things on them is important. We need to let them continue to solve their own problems and not jump in to save the day.

While visiting, turn the strategy around by letting them practice being adults. Having them do things for themselves is key. Cleaning up their own dishes, doing their own laundry, and pointing out that they need to be sure to pick up their own shoes and items are what need to be addressed.

Little reminders and hints that they are adults living on their own can help to put them back into their new mindset. They will also have that melancholy feeling and may want to regress. Simply treating them like any adult staying in your home is the answer.

Mindset is a powerful aspect. The more you practice seeing your children for the age they are, the more you will treat them as such. Of course it's fine to help them with their laundry or prepare their favorite meal. Be sure not to once again become the mom of a grade schooler when, in fact, they are a college student.

By treating your children as an adult, you are now able to have adult conversations. When they were younger, your children were seeking security from their parents. Now that they are grown, they may still seek comfort. It is time to do this on a new level. While doing so, remember that they will have different opinions about life now. Be sure to be neutral giving them the freedom to voice their opinion on a subject.

If a friend had a problem with their finances, you wouldn't just pay their way, you'd help them figure out strategies to take care of it themselves. As parents to grown children, we need to do the same thing. Parents can begin to practice reaching out to their grown children the same way they would any other adult by listening, showing compassion, and being helpful.

After you start to relate to them in this adult fashion, they begin to feel adult security and rely on your helpful hints instead of doing it for them. Take it from someone who has been there, it really is a wonderful feeling to have independent, hard working, adult children that became so once you changed your mindset.

17

Stay Connected with Common Interests

When my younger daughter lived at home, Saturday night would be the beginning of her and her dad's ritual. Tara would start mixing her cookie batter, usually chocolate chip, and locate her favorite plastic container to put them in. Since she was a volleyball player at about 5'11", she could always reach up and grab what she needed in the kitchen. Her dad would begin rearranging the surfboards out back to get to them easier in the morning.

While the cookies would bake, both Tara and her dad would collect the wetsuits they would need depending on the water temperature, pull down some beach towels from the linen closet upstairs, and lay out their surf watches. Tara's was a birthday gift from her older sister that had a shark fin that moved across the face of the watch. You could feel the energy they shared for the sport and each other as they went about collecting their toys for tomorrow's dawn patrol. After the cookies cooled, she would select the bikini she would wear and try to go to bed early.

Dawn patrol would start pretty early in the morning at our house. The morning began with her dad walking into her bedroom and whispering it was time. It was like listening to little mice tiptoeing from the upstairs bedrooms and bathroom to downstairs where they would be pouring their coffee into their favorite to-go travel mugs. They would select their boards based on the swell mentioned when checking the surf report.

You could hear the front door open and them leaning their boards against the house as they carried their surf box that had towels, wetsuits, coffee, and cookies. Tara carried the surf box while her dad carried both their boards to the surf mobile, our 1994 Ford Bronco with surf racks. A few times I would sneak out of bed and watch from the upstairs balcony of our condo as the pair headed out to do their favorite thing together.

As they headed out, I would think how is he going to handle it when she follows in her sister's footsteps and heads to college soon? How is my husband going to handle the absence of his surfing buddy when she heads off to school? I better start thinking of alternatives for him because I know for sure that I don't want to learn how to surf!

When Tara was searching for her college, she researched the colleges that would best offer her an MBA while rewarding her with the most scholarship funds and where she could continue to play volleyball. After a prolonged research, she was the top recruited volleyball player with about 90% full ride scholarship at her chosen university. I loved that the location was on the east coast near a few popular surf spots. Once she was settled in and began walking around, she found a surf shop and was sure to talk to her dad about it.

Some mornings on the weekends, she would go out to the surf spots and take some video sending them to her dad. They'd talk about what it looked like and what wetsuit thickness she'd need to wear because the water temperature was so cold back East compared to CA. For Christmas, her dad loved opening gifts wrapped from Tara that had a t-shirt or hat from the surf shop down the road from her dorm.

When our surfing buddies move away, it is up to us as the parent to keep the interest going. Because of their dawn patrols every Sunday morning started when she was 11, they had a special bond in that routine. The key was that they continued to nurture that bond even though she was 3,000 miles away. Whenever spotting a post on Facebook of a surf contest or video of surfers, her dad always made a point of sharing it with her.

As a result, there is no need to end the connection, but rather elevate its importance. Whatever shared interest you have with your college student, keep the flames burning by reaching out and speaking about it. Even if it's to reminisce about the fun times, make the call and let them know you remembered that awesome wave that they took off on a few years back. (Surfers are like baseball fans who remember what player was on first twenty years prior.)

Of course when our children venture off to start their life at college, it's our time to recall the fun, remind our kids how much it meant to us, and continue the connection; that's all our kids, I mean adults, really want.

18

Gather Their Accomplishments and Frame Them

As you look for items that you need in different places like the junk dresser and desk drawers in your house, the more you'll come across those swim medals, sports awards, and trophies that your college kids have left behind. From my experience, these were found everywhere as I cleaned up and boxed up their favorite things. However, as we sit in this new phase of being an empty nester, we find we have time to think about what to do with them. A great productive project that can be very loving to your heart is taking all their accomplishments and putting them into frames. But as we miss them, how do we go about doing this?

When the months tick on, there's more time to think of the life that we created when our children were still in the nest.

All the favorite times we had will come trickling into mind. Now that they've flown off, we feel a bit lost. With all this time, we can go into all those drawers, nooks, and crannies throughout their room and pull out all their favorite awards and achievements. Have fun with this idea by reliving the fun parts of attending all those sporting events.

Maybe start by getting a box to put in all their accolades. Be sure to treat this as fun. As awards are found, take time to remember dates and mark them. Possibly find photos that go along with the special moment. We all have those in our phones. This is a good time to not only review all their feats, but also all the hard work you put in to help them achieve those accomplishments.

As I began boxing sweatshirts and other clothing for different times of the year for them, I came across their awards or recognition from their swim team moments, volleyball, and surfing. It was fun to remember all those fun times going to volleyball tournaments in Los Angeles, Phoenix, and Vegas. When I hunted through my phone for pictures, it was like opening a treasure chest of the best moments of being a parent.

Since one daughter was more organized, she had her awards all together. By going through my drawers, I found other tickets, programs, and doodads that would look great in frames. Be sure to take advantage of the craft store's coupons. We would buy one frame at a time to save money. Laying these out in their frame was special for us to reminisce all these precious times, as well as create important keepsakes.

This is a great idea because it helps us transform our sadness into fun. It is a wonderful time to remember all the great times and the ones that made them the strong individuals that they became.

In addition, it helps us stay out of complete sadness by realizing how our parenting was key to helping them progress. When our children leave the nest, there is no award of recognition given to us, so this is a great way to give ourselves one. As you hang these prizes up on the walls of your empty nest, it will give you comfort and pride in all their efforts and capabilities.

19

Make Care Packages for the Holidays

We all want to feel loved. By collecting fun holiday things and sending them to your kids who flew the nest, you can send your love to them through the mail. When they were home, you made sure they received some fun goodies as the holidays came around. Now is the time to fill our own bucket by filling theirs with some of their favorites.

By flying the coop, our chick-a-dees can be several hours away and if they select a college on another coast or even in another country, they won't always be able to come home for holiday celebrations. Simply take time to shop stores to find objects that fit their personality and taste.

Be sure to pick up a box from the Post Office that allows delivery in 3-4 days. As you pick up groceries, take time to look over the holiday items available. Since our stores seem to have these goods out way before the date, it is easy to include these purchases into your budget.

If you think back, when you went off to school or moved away, you were homesick every now and then. I remember receiving a call or letter and how it would brighten my day. When we step back into that time, it can help us to connect with how our children might be feeling and how we can make an impact.

There's nothing like receiving a parcel. Just knowing that someone was thinking of you and went out of their way is the best feeling. No matter what you send, it will mean the world to them.

When my girls attended college, the universities had a contract with a company that would put together boxes of items for holidays. Because they were expensive and didn't have their favorites, I put these boxes together myself.

I would find cute socks, candles, note pads, and candy to mark the occasion. Since one liked skulls and the other sharks, I always kept my eyes out for those types of items. When in a store that sells things for a dollar, I'm always sure to purchase name brand candy or get them at the grocery store. Even a little note tucked in the box has always brought thank you texts with heart exclamation marks.

At the end of the college school year, there are those dreaded exams. Although we used the school's company that would send coffee, hot chocolate and different snack foods, we made sure to send other things, like one's Surfer or Food Network magazine, and their favorite snacks.

We could always hear the excitement in their voice during a call or see their big smile as they FaceTime with us. With all the stress that comes with those exams, helping them feel a little love and a little bit of home with these mailings can alleviate some of the pressure and stress.

I hope you take the time to send your love. This is a great way to remind your children where their original nest exists. Send them boxes full of your love with all their favorites. To them, it's like a little bit of home in their new space. Not only does this show your love, but it keeps the lines of communication open. Sometimes the box doesn't even have to come with a holiday. Sometimes we send a bunch of seasonings when they request a certain sweatshirt to keep them warm. Tucking in some of their favorite recipes of what I used to make them is pure love.

20

Find Your Smile Again

The worst thing to see is the fake smile of someone trying to look happy or merely trying to get through a discussion. A business partner did that, and all you could see were his teeth framed by his lips. In actuality, if we use our energy for good and not evil, our smiles can transform everybody and everything.

Researchers at the University of Kansas published findings that when we smile, it reduces the body's response to stress. It actually lowers the heart rate and blood pressure in tense situations. As a matter of fact, it can lead to longevity. Now that we're empty nesters, it's time to get our smile on and live life to the fullest.

Back in the 19th century, a scientist named Guillaume Duchenne found that a true smile is composed of two sets of important muscles, the zygomatic and the orbicularis oculi. As these raise the corners of the mouth and raise the cheeks forming crow's feet around the eyes, it is said that you are indeed smiling with joy.

The data revealed that a true "Duchenne smile" was produced by an area in the brain's left anterior temporal where they found connections to positive affect. In fact, during a 30 year study, research shows that people with Duchenne-worthy expressions have greater levels of general well-being and a happier marriage when in their 50's. This goes to show that genuine smiles are people showing their core disposition.

After a fierce downpour at our home during the Covid 19 lockdown, I would have to agree with these findings. As neighbors were gathering to help one neighbor with hoses to help drain water levels rising, I could totally see my neighbor's true core spirit.

Even when the rain was creating such a negative outcome for my neighbor, he smiled from ear to ear as we switched shoes. Because he was wearing bags on his shoes and I had tall rain boots on, I told him to wear mine. As he helped pull them off my feet while standing in the downpour, we just laughed. Nonetheless, he put them on and I walked home barefoot. Hearing him laugh and joining in made the situation even more bearable. Here we all were sheltering in place afraid to be near others, yet everyone came to the rescue.

As you already know as a parent, as soon as your child sees you smile at them, they smile back. They definitely possess a Duchenne Smile because you're their soul. Peggy Mason, a neurobiologist from the University of Chicago, found results from her study that smiles are contagious and help us connect. She found that when using our smiles, we create a kind of "social cohesion" that enables us to feel empathy and help one another to survive.

Indeed, with outcomes and findings like that, who wouldn't want to smile? If I can lower my blood pressure, heart rate, and connect with others by showing my core spirit, of course I'm going to show my true smile from ear to ear. The best findings are that they found those with a true Duchenne smile actually had the calmest hearts. Not only can your smile become contagious, but you just might very well be helping to calm those in your presence. I guess Barry Manilow had it right when he sang, "I Can't Smile Without You!"

21

Visit Places You Kept Putting Off

We are all aware that when we put our mind on something else, we can't think of things that bring us down. Why not start putting your mind on saving a little bit of money and start collecting some vacation brochures? What a great time to think back to all those places you always wanted to visit. There are even local places to think about visiting if financial resources are at a minimum.

As you think of places to visit, think of ways to pay for your trip. Since our girls went to college back East, we always made sure to collect their miles. In order to increase ours we started using a credit card that offered miles for every dollar. We would pay some of our monthly bills with the card in order to accumulate miles. Be sure to make payments in full every month to avoid getting into debt.

The internet has many virtual tours to look at to determine where to visit. Simply Google interesting vacation spots and have a date night going over all the places you imagined going. Maybe as a child, you always dreamed of walking the Wall of China and to eat authentic Chinese food. Now is a great time to put your focus on something positive like this.

Since we know that we can only have one thought at a time, it's time to manage our thoughts to be positive. We can very easily fall into a slump feeling sad and thinking of how much we miss our kids. It's a perfect time to stay positive and consider where to travel. Going to see sights nearby is a great idea. By reviewing the history of your city or state, you can find exciting spots to see. If you review the cost, have the amount on the refrigerator and mirror of the bathroom to keep your focus on your goal. Just as we go to stress eat, we'll see our plan and hopefully it will deter us from having that extra snack.

Whenever we went back East for our family vacation, we enjoyed seeing a new lighthouse each time. Now I have a chance to locate and tour some on the West Coast. Some are right in my backyard of San Diego County where I can take a day trip. Others are north and south of San Francisco where we can reserve a hotel and look for interesting restaurants right on the water's edge.

First take a virtual tour and notice which ones you'd like to see up close. Take notice of other activities or features near the lighthouse to make your trip fun-filled. American history is a favorite subject of my spouse's, so we can have something for both tastes; a lighthouse for me and a historic spot for him.

As stated before, a visit to a historic place would be something for my spouse. I could locate a waterfall, hiking locations, and possible campgrounds to keep the cost down and the adventure up. Now that our daughters are back East we could continue our lighthouse tour back there.

Since we miss seeing them, we could plan a time when everyone is available to do some weekend traveling. We can use our miles accrued from our card and enjoy getting some well-deserved time with our girls. Massachusetts and Philadelphia are filled with history. It would be fun to learn new things while getting to spend time with our daughters.

What better way to save for a vacation than by receiving miles simply by making your own bill payments. By selecting interesting places we've always wanted to visit since we were kids, we can now actually enjoy them. If we're smart, we can find some marvelous places near our daughters that would have new features. Therefore, not only would we be filling our hearts from seeing our girls, but we'd be fulfilling an old childhood dream as well. Once we get the hang of saving for such outings, maybe we can plan a trip that includes the whole family.

22

Buy the Crunchy Peanut Butter

When you enter the empty nest stage, you will probably take an enormous inhale and exhale. There will be a moment where you become aware of all your sacrifices. It is time to take a few breaths, kick your feet up, and enjoy the play back in your mind of each and every one of them. As they come up one by one, be sure to pull out the ones you want back.

Parenting comes with sacrifice. It changes everything from what you can afford to everything they want. However, the silver lining of being an empty nester is that you now have the option of taking back those things you always loved, but put on the back burner.

Of course we had to trade having our nails done to purchasing bulk diapers or formula, but even the small things had to be removed. Despite some sadness of missing our children, we get to bring our favorites back into the nest.

Because you've gone so long without favorites, it might feel a bit weird to see them back in your life. It is absolutely noteworthy to start your collection again. Not only will they bring a happy feeling, but they remind you time and again of all you've done for your children. Giving up things for others was very honorable.

As my children came home for visits, they would see crunchy style peanut butter instead of creamy in the cupboard. It certainly drummed up discussions of when and why that changed from the normal jar they were accustomed to seeing. Since they're older and wiser on these visits, hopefully it is a small lesson to them on how lucky they are to have had such a wonderfully thoughtful mother.

As my children grew up, many of my favorites were sidelined since my wallet only held so much. Since I couldn't create a pantry that looked like an aisle at the local grocery store that included all the different peanut butter and jellies I sacrificed what I liked for what they wanted.

One of my favorites was crunchy peanut butter. I loved the little pieces of peanut in every taste, but since my little ones weren't big fans, I bought what they enjoyed. Funny how putting my favorite crunchy peanut butter back in the pantry and on my bread put a smile to my face.

It's amazing how once you put back even the smallest cherished treasure into your life, your heart feels replenished. Maybe it's going without something so meaningful for so long that helps us feel accomplished. Finding time to get back on my bike, sit at the beach when I want to, or spread the crunchy peanut butter on a soft piece of bread helps us see just how far we went to be a successful parent.

Whether it's a jar of crunchy peanut butter or the top of the line bourbon, it's time to take back your life by bringing in positive energy. Although we understand why we sacrificed our wants, we need to give our soul something to smile about. When sadness creeps back into our mind, what better time to think about how darn amazing of a mom you were by changing even the littlest thing for your little ones' hearts.

23

Reconnect with Friends & Family

Who knew? All those years ago when I would write my pen pal in CA from NY, I was doing something for my mental and physical health by increasing happiness along with reducing stress. In addition to promoting health, writing letters are more tangible, and they're the perfect act of kindness. It's a lost art form hopefully with a comeback ahead.

We all have phones with the capabilities of texting messages. Gone are the days where we put exciting life changing events into a call or letter. Now anything from an engagement to splitting up your assets is done over a text and not done by voice or letter.

By connecting with friends and family with letters, it is something that someone can actually hold and display. What if someone told you it would reduce your stress and make you feel happier? Would you try it? Why not have a go at it?

No meds to ingest and no specialty doctor visit, just a simple piece of paper with words.

With our printers nowadays, we can create our own stationery. We can even pick up some adorable all occasion cards at the local store. As we write from the heart, we are sharing our vulnerability with others. We are taking time to be still and write our true feelings. What better way to relax than by having comforting words come to mind. When we receive a text, we can't very well display it on the shelf in the living room in order to see it every day to remind us that someone thought of you. A simple act of kindness can put a smile on someone's face.

As a kid, I wrote letters to a friend I met in CA at the age of ten. Now at 58 years young, we finally live in the same state. At various parties, we talk about how much fun we had sharing what was going on in our lives that young. When I went to England as an exchange student, I received many letters from family and friends. I'm glad I was smart enough to put them in an old shoe box for safe keeping. Until this day, I can still look at those wonderful words of encouragement.

Every year many of us join in the tradition of sending Christmas cards. In our house, for the longest time this wonderful family friend would always be the first person to send hers. It's now an honor in our household to be the one who sends us the first card. Not only does it put a smile on our face, but it really helps us see how grateful we are for our friends.

As a child, I had another friend send a card on my birthday or a cute card just to make me smile. Even though she lived right up the hill, she always put her feelings into words for me. Today, I still have a smile on my face when she sends any holiday card at any season. She even sends me one thanking me for my friendship. One day she shared with me that by sending me that message of gratuity, it helped her when she was feeling lost and low.

Since having to be sheltered in place, we've all learned the importance of friends and family. How wonderful would it be to use the postal service for more than sending payments for bills? I know from experience how my heart fills with love when I received a letter from across the pond as a young college student or even across the country today.

Receiving these letters and cards was always like seeing their soul. Since it's a way of sharing your feelings, it is a wonderful act of kindness to both your heart and the one holding it. Now that our schedule allows us time for letter writing, why not try to be part of a new trend introducing an old idea. Without a doubt, what a great way to help us empty nesters fill our hearts and empty nests by simply using this great way to create love and communicate that love for ourselves and others.

PART THREE

Getting Started On Your New Life

24

List Your Goals & Focus on Accomplishing Them

One of my favorite things to do is make a list. Whether it is for grocery shopping, house cleaning or my writing, it's always been a life saver. Some say a goal without a plan is only a wish. The plan itself and then writing down the goal helps it become realized. Our goals help us move forward with motivation. On the path, it keeps us accountable while also setting our priorities. Alas, we can look back and see our progress. Now that we start our new stage as an empty nester, it's time to sit still and start writing them.

Find a quiet place and sit with the thought of you. Ask yourself questions such as, "What do I want to do with my new found time?" "What are some things that I always wanted to accomplish at this age?" And, "What were my hopes and dreams when becoming an adult with adult children?" Be honest with yourself and jot down all your feelings and ideas.

Out of these, you can start your plan to help you move forward. So many parents get stuck in this stage of becoming an empty nester. They feel like they need to become similar to the beefeater guard waiting for any problem from their grown children to occur and rush to the rescue. At the top of your list, be sure to write: Adult children can handle their own problems - Time for me to live my life!

Because some parents stay on the sidelines waiting to be needed, they get stuck and can't move forward. Once you move forward in this stage, many possibilities begin to spring up like daffodils. Create a plan for your goals that includes things that you enjoy and see how it helps to inspire you. When these goals are set in a schedule, it helps to keep us motivated. As you look over the list of goals you've made, you can prioritize them by how you want your end results to occur.

For example, if you are going to have guests show up in a short amount of time, prioritize what their needs are then work on the wants. As you begin these steps towards your goals, you will see the transformation you made to your own life. You are filling it with truly meaningful aspects that create happiness and joy inside. In a short period of time, you can look back and compare this new schedule with the lonely one you would have had if not for that day of answering those questions based on you.

I remember the first few weekends were spent relaxing and not rushing off to our children's sports events. When we realized how much time and effort we put into that time, we were proud of our accomplishments, but then noticed that we now had time for our own interests.

Since no one is exactly the same, we made sure we started filling our time with things we enjoyed separately. Scheduling time with girlfriends, going back to a book club, and breaking out the ol' bike helped motivate me. It became noticeable to us all the work that was put off on our home. Now was the time to fix and replace old appliances, broken overhangs, and tending to the yard and garden. We had fun picking out items that we liked and working together in the yard. It also became very noticeable how we didn't have to tend to making others' meals and had fun tending to us.

Because my dream was to always write books, it was a tremendous feeling to put that center stage on my list. Since my husband loved fixing cars, he enjoyed the relaxing feeling of working on the family cars, but more importantly his surf mobile. By doing the things we liked, it moved us out of the sadness of missing our children. We found it fun to talk about them to the kids on our calls. It was definitely a learning moment for them to seek their favorite things and vise versa. We started sharing our choices with them. Even apart from them, we can still be that teaching force modeling how to create goals and follow through.

With just a piece of paper and pen, you can take your sadness from missing your children and replace it with fun things to accomplish. It is useful to schedule certain weekends even though you can change and reposition their priority. Having goals for home improvements as well as self improvement should both have a place on your list. Occasionally, sit back after a few months and look at all your progress.

You will notice that by simply creating goals, you helped yourself move through the sadness of having an empty nest. I point out that now you have a nest all to yourself with time ahead of you to spice it up. Let your goals become your friend and be sure to place your favorites in between the must-dos

25

Learn Something New

Who says old dogs can't learn new tricks? What better time to learn something new than when you no longer have to cart everyone to school or their sporting events. In your new empty nest, it's time to think back to all the things you've always wanted to learn and get cracking. It is a perfect time to fill your brain with new information you've always wanted to learn.

As your birds fly the coop, you might feel strange and a bit out of your comfort zone when it comes to learning something new. In fact, this is the ideal time to start. If you look around, you may notice the change in technology keeps on improving. There's nothing like the present to get up to date. Not only is it a great time to learn new things, but just using your brain creates new synapses and improves your ability to learn. This can get us empty nesters hooked on learning and make it a lifelong process.

Every time we learn something new, our brain changes in a significant way. We can actually improve our memory, verbal and language skills, as well as develop a productive failure skill where we are encouraged to fail knowing we are learning. Maybe we want to learn a new language or a new skill? With these benefits for our brain, it certainly is a good time to learn anything you've always dreamed of knowing.

A friend told me how she was taking a course on flying drones. Included in the learning, she studied FAA rules as well as weather in order to grasp the drone knowledge. Here is a perfect example of learning something from our fast changing technology. Because so many companies are starting to use drones to survey service for roofs, delivery service, and inspections of all kinds, now is the best time to learn something that is quickly becoming very popular.

Many of us have always dreamt of visiting a foreign country. With our new available time, empty nesters can learn the language of the area they always wanted to visit. While learning the new language, find places in your community where you can practice your contemporary skill. There are many online software courses that can help you attain this new language. What a great way of meeting new friends too

Learning something new is the best thing for your brain. For this reason, not only will you improve its growth, but now it can help you meet new people while grasping a new concept. You can join the updated world of technology, attain a new language, and gain new friendships. By putting your mind on something very important to you, your health improves in the process. Having a happy and healthy body and mind is the goal during this new empty nest stage. This is a great lesson to your children as well. When they get to this stage themselves, they'll know what to do from following your lead.

26

Create a New Relationship with your Spouse

If I'm completely honest, I have put this chapter off many times. When I attempted to begin, it started in so many different ways. Interestingly enough, some thoughts started off very excited while others began with a warning that this could possibly make or break your connection with your significant other.

After reading through the various notes I jotted down, it all comes to the same conclusion. It's time to create something new. The word 'new' is the key. It won't go back to what you once had, however it can become the greatest thing ever.

At this point, it is a must to approach this chapter slowly but with enthusiasm. My first piece of advice would be to simply sit down together having some nice appetizers and beverages and start talking about how you met, remembering when the kids were little, and how quickly it all went. Secondly, I'd actually speak another time on what you both want in your relationship now that the nest is empty.

Whether you find yourself bickering or not, this is a great time to find a marriage counselor or therapist who can help you find your way back to each other. If we're honest with ourselves, we have been growing in different directions from the time our new college freshmen were tiny tots. Even though you may have accomplished having date nights every month for the past eighteen years, it is time to sit down and work out your feelings by laying them down on the table.

During this long journey of raising children, parents need a refresher course on how to make the other parent a priority, how to communicate, when it's best to schedule a discussion, and how to be consistent in all these new areas. Just like my four keys in Parenting Scholar Athletes, it's important to sprinkle LOVE into each area of discussion to help make it work.

While we were learning how to raise student athletes and rushing here and there, we may not have had much time for anything else, but it is now time to learn how to look at our bad habits and replace them with good ones.

Obviously, we've all done it. We have all learned bad habits and how to push the other's buttons in a negative way. We're not perfect, but we have a chance to work on becoming the couple we want to be as our children are learning to be the responsible adults they want to be.

Because a person goes through life's lessons and significant events, such as losing family members, it is easy to realize that we learned how to shut off our feelings. Now is the perfect time to simply remember the love we have for the person who is the love of our life.

Since we found ourselves arguing with no solution, we read Everybody Wins by Gary Chapman. It helped us understand the difference between arguing and having a conflict that can have a solution. In the interest of staying together, we began verbalizing how we felt. In doing so, we realized we weren't listening to each other. More importantly we learned that we can have a "re-do" if we notice we made a mistake.

I highly recommend these strategies because nothing is worth more than rekindling the love you have for your significant other. After all that was said and done, finding a counselor we both appreciated and trusted helped get us back on the road of enjoying each other and having an empty nest full of love and fun!

27

Take Care of the Honey-Do List

That first look around is the most powerful. As a parent of scholar athletes, we were putting all our effort into their sports and schools. They had different activity practices and early morning study sessions to get to each week during middle & high school. Every weekend consisted of tournament travel, meals, parking, and more meals.

Since our time was being used for their activities, we had no free time to get anything done. Not only that, but we had been pumping all our funds into their needs. On one hand there were sports fees, then each weekend sport tournaments not to mention the money for gear and travel expenses as well. Once they moved to NCAA colleges, the gear became even more expensive. But then there was that light at the end of the tunnel.

As our efforts ended because they were off to college, the view was like looking at the aftermath of a storm. Mouth fully opens in amazement as you turn your head side to side in each room of your home. However, it is sweet when the work starts. Seeing your home being put back into place is the ultimate feeling. Of course, a plan has to be made.

The best plan is to go room by room and list the work that should be completed. Next, by using a calendar for scheduling different jobs, mark weekends and evenings with projects allotted for that time. When all areas are looked at and put on the calendar to accomplish, take time to collect the supplies little by little.

Now with a plan, be sure to schedule more than enough time to finish each job with an ample amount of rest in between. There will be painting of walls that have aged carpet that has seen better days, and closets that need a whole new transformation. Look at this as a special time full of positive energy being put back into your space. Although considerable changes like your children leaving the nest are still quite new in the air, think of this as an important new stage where this renewal phase is your graduation from the old to the new.

Beautiful moments from the past will find their way back in sight as you remove and go through used and tattered belongings you once stowed in your closet. These photos and mementos will take you back to a time to show you how far you've come. Seeing the smiling faces from past vacation snapshots will bring a warm feeling to your heart. They will expose just how much you've grown as a parent and person.

One area we worked on was our closet. For years, that was where everything was tucked away as we got the house ready for Christmas and the kids coming home. Since we didn't have the funds to do a whole new closet redesigning, we kept shoving more crap into the empty spots. Once we started taking these bags and boxes out, it was a wonderful release. Some questions that came to mind were, "Why did we keep this?" "Where did this come from?" And then acknowledging, "Oh, there's where that went!" There's the fun of finding old Christmas gifts that were never given because they were lost in the world of the closet. Likewise, there's the fun of finding old photos that bring a smile with great memories to mind.

Not only is it a great time to throw away all the things that had no more use, but it's a great feeling to let these things go while opening up new space. At first there may be discussions about keeping certain items but remember what Marie Kondo would say, "Does it bring joy?" I found that taking a picture of some things helped detach. Remind yourself that it may take more time than planned and remember we're not as young as we used to be. Keep moving forward even if it means doing just a small amount each evening.

The second project didn't start for a few years. Because the girls studied at their universities back East, it was hard to redecorate in their room. I feel we kept everything the same in order to help us feel better. Once they stopped returning home during the summers when they graduated, that was when it hit us to modify their old space to meet our needs. Through a few Christmas and summer visits, they went through their clothes and belongings. All we had to do was purchase long shallow containers that would fit under their beds to put their mementos.

On a beautiful visit to Hawaii arranged by our girls, we found some lovely art that we hung in the room as we began to make it the guest room. Once we did that, the rest began to flow through completion. It was interesting how the ideas we had as young parents popped up and made their way out again. The area may emulate a road construction project for a bit, however it is worth the time and mess.

The unveiling of our former selves was what we found during this lesson. As we found old photos and mementos, we could feel how much we had grown since those old ideas that once bounced around in our heads. It is amazing how the old thoughts and hair styles help us realize how much we've grown as adults.

The worries of raising our children wrong and not doing things correct were all a thing of the past. We realized how the things of the past are really nothing to lose sleep over. Seeing how much we've grown added to the importance of creating this old space of theirs into a new space for us. Admiring the new art will always remind us of the family vacations in Hawaii as well as the generous gift of returning there thanks to our kids.

At this point, we've found how important it is to not let things get to us. For instance, after all this time we realized that we were correct to not compete with the Jones'. We did things the way we needed to fit our family and we can say so long to the younger version of ourselves.

Talk about coming full circle. Since we are in the same house where we started our family, it is amazing to see how many transformations their room went through. At the beginning, it was an extra room when we first married. Once the children were born, the floor went from carpet to linoleum. As they grew older, carpet returned to help with the noise and the walls had a few different colors. Now it is being transformed into a guest room again with our fun toys like a large screen TV and room for a yoga mat.

As the work was accomplished, I could see the older version of myself sitting in the rocking chair with the babies wondering what will become of them. This strategy was the most fulfilling. It was amazing to see them accomplish their dreams as well as seeing how far I've come and just how fast it all went. When you are able to look back and not feel sad any more, you will be able to look forward to your own dreams and be open to all the possibilities.

28

Get Out of the House and Explore

It is essential to get out doors and into the sunshine soaking up as much vitamin D as possible. We've also found that exploring places we are familiar with is crucial. When you enter this empty nest stage, your feelings and emotions keep you stuck. The main thing is to pump up your mind and find some ways to take those first steps.

Being in a new stage of life makes a person want to remain where they feel safe. Disconnecting from that secure place is hard on the mind and body and the longer you stay in that safe space, the harder it is to change to take that step.

Thinking back to Covid times, it was a bit scary to go back to places like a grocery store. There were new rules like wearing masks, following the signs on the floor for proper distancing, and seeing clear plastic shields at every cashier station. If you think back, it was hard to get used to these changes. This is the same thing when you enter this empty nest stage. Without having those scheduled chores, you feel a bit lonely and no meaning to your day. It's time to think of things that appeal to you to help get you out the door.

When I would think of what a self- help book might contain, I was under the impression that it included using the higher levels of our brain. As I began reading certain ones to help me in a particular situation, I was always blown away on how easy or down to earth the solutions were. It had nothing to do with splitting the atom or doing brain surgery. I found that the best answers were always those with the most common sense. Venturing out by taking small steps sounds so easy and you're probably asking yourself why you didn't think of that on your own. But isn't that part of the answer too? Sometimes we are so far into a problem and have dug ourselves so deep that the easy answers seem to have slipped right out of our thoughts. As you hear these strategies, give yourself a break from judgments, think of the ones that stir up an excitement within you, and make a plan to use them.

Thinking of venturing out on a walk might make your brain suddenly come up with several excuses not to go. Isn't that the part of our brain that we love the most? We love its ability to help us out of something we don't want to do. In order to help us sidestep that negative part, it's important to make your plan simple. A reminder that a simple walk has nothing to do with preparing for the Olympics is a good start and a great way to think. I think about an easy route to take and only doing it for the smallest amount of time possible.

Take your phone and as you walk outside, set your timer for 10 minutes and begin to walk in your neighborhood. Knowing that it is only a short time will help your mind agree. As you walk, make an agreement with yourself that you're only going to think of positive things. Literally have a few ideas ready because our minds like to take over and be in control. For instance, I make ready memories of me enjoying Hawaii and fishing in Maine. If my mind goes to thinking of my girls and starts to worry, I force myself to think of one of my choices. Since I can't think of a negative idea as I'm thinking of a positive one, I'm winning. Sometimes I would find myself going a bit further when my alarm would sound. But know it is not a negative thing to immediately turn for home as you hear the chimes. When you arrive home, be sure to pat yourself on the back and immediately think of all the great things you saw on your walk. Because you make it fun for your body and mind, you'll find yourself wanting to do it more often and walk farther.

While errands have to be done, be sure to set them up the same way you did with your new walking idea. Make it fun by doing it with your spouse and penciling a stop off for a favorite drink or time to browse a fun local vinyl store. (For all you young whippersnappers, that's a record store.) I found doing my errands with my spouse made it fun. As we talked through the boring shopping, it seemed to get done quicker. Even if I would venture off on my own, it was fun to stop off for a healthy smoothie. "Two birds", as my dad would say.

In order to feel unstuck from the empty nest feeling, explore new places by leaving your favorite stop for last. Then it will feel like a reward for all your hard work. Flipping through the vinyl at an old record shop or looking through your favorite hobby store, you'll find your mind having a ball! It reminds us how to make time for all our loves. Keeping your mind on things that bring a smile to your face is what's crucial. It is essential to separate the negative feelings going on inside your head and put the spotlight on all the fun things you love instead.

Now the most important thing is to put this all into action. Get your planner out and schedule a short walk. Pick a time in the next day or two, find some comfortable walking clothes and shoes, and start thinking of all those positive memories to store in your brain. One of the most effective ways I have prepared for my walks is to literally set out my clothes and shoes.

In addition, set up a time to do errands and be sure to schedule your favorite store at the end. From stopping at a cooking store to swinging by a sporting shop, start planning out your next move and enjoy.

29

Declutter Your Nest

Downsizing in this chapter refers to storing those items of meaning for your children, preparing your space to rearrange later, or for possible moving. At this point, downsizing also refers to tidying up and releasing items that are no longer needed. My first recommendation is to invest in Marie Kondo's book, The Life-Changing Magic of Tidying Up. If it's videos you like, there's many online where she shares her tips and knowledge. She has a wonderful way of presenting any problem with wonderful solutions to organizing and decluttering.

Your nest may be partially empty since your children took some of their belongings with them, and there are probably things of theirs that still remain. For the sake of this chapter, we're going to speak about organizing, decluttering, collecting valuables, giving unwanted items away, and storing items that bring joy.

Be sure to go into this phase in a calm manner. If this project is done with unhappiness, there will be an outcome not befitting this phase. Embark on this in a celebrating manner. With today's technology, you can have your kids take part with you as you sort through items and belongings.

By using the recommended categories that Marie Kondo advises, you can FaceTime your child. They can help you realize what to get rid of, what is a keepsake to them, and what to put aside for them to look at on their next visit. From my experience, actually scheduling time for their organizing on their next visit home works.

Because downsizing has three different ways of sorting which are discard, give away, and keep, I started using Marie Kondo's wisdom and practice on each. Go into this project knowing that it will take time. No need to rush and discard something that brings them joy.

It is said that this can be hard on parents because they may want to keep everything. As you work in different categories of clothing, books, and papers, simply start with the items that are clearly broken and not useful. Next, gather their important award certificates and cute letters written and put in a safe place for them to review. Last, see the room as a new space for you to enjoy life.

Although one daughter told me to just throw out everything except a few things, I still sorted and left the throwing out to be done by her on the next visit home. Because I didn't want to feel bad for discarding something important to her, I waited and let her have the privilege. My other daughter actually went through her clothes and created two give away bags. She looked over her personal childhood toys and put them into plastic bins to use later for her own children one day.

Be sure not to look into the bags they fill and tie for the thrift store. It really does create a flood of emotions that come over you. As your brain reminds you, spinning each memory into your mind and heart, it's probably not a good idea to peek. Remind yourself they made the decision and choice, so it must be trusted. This is the same trust that I practice when reviewing their objects. It isn't up to me to throw away the things that bring them joy.

By doing this project with someone logical who can take the same care as you is wise. Remind yourself that it doesn't have to be accomplished that day. We purchased plastic bins that were long, but not too high, so it would fit under their twin beds. You'll be amazed how much these bins hold.

Practice your trust by not reading diaries or letters that are not for you. It is their private items that have special meaning to them. If you want them to have these papers and mementos, stick them in a postal box. As you see progress start thinking of ways you can use the space. This will help you follow through to completion because now you have a goal. By knowing that you will get to use this space for something fun, this feeling will help you finish this project.

Downsizing helps everyone remember the important things in life. By creating open space to enjoy, we realize we do not fill every space we have or live in a paycheck-work-spend cycle. It is certainly a wonderful time to express gratitude for the time these items were here and the love they brought. This helps our children live less attached to stuff. When it is their turn to get rid of things after college each year, they'll have this experience to draw from. May this time help you appreciate more, spend less, and find joy in items you want to bring into this space.

30

Rearrange Your Nest

Now that you've gone through the process of declutter and organization, it is a great time to rearrange your nest to fit your needs. Refrain from using it as a storage area. When your children lived in this space, it wasn't storage so make good use of it. Keep this sacred space for something fun and nurturing for you to use.

Sometimes it is hard to take this step. If you don't jump right to this stage, have no regrets. It simply means you're not ready for this phase. It takes time to move through their things and think of how to move the furniture around.

As parents, we want to keep everything the same way because it might help us feel like they are still here. But that only takes away the time and space that could be used for you. There are different ways to use this space. By discussing out loud how to use it, we can see it can have a new purpose Your thoughts may try to come up with reasons to keep it the same; however it is important to realize it can all be repositioned if they return home.

As they live their new lives, they don't live for that space anymore. Think of it as their parting gift to you. It might feel weird at first, but move forward. Create ideas, think of changes such as paint and flooring, and most importantly use the space for you. Maybe you enjoy sewing, scrapbooking, or exercising. This is the perfect time to figure out what you really want out of life and go for it. When you venture out on a trip, maybe bring that place home with you in the form of art. By having these new pictures to look at while doing your favorite hobby, it adds positivity to your life. But, of course, have the room redesigned so that it can be a guest room ready for your children's next visit.

I have to admit, it took me a few years to do this one. Because they went to college on the East Coast, I only saw them on Christmas and then for the summer months. Since they were scholar athletes, they always left early in August for pre-season workouts.

Lying on their beds seeing the perspective from their end was fun. Their cats loved sleeping on their beds. However, my husband & I started coming around. Each time they came home, we had them go through their things. They were good about going through their clothes and weeding out the ones for the thrift store. I even saw things bagged for the trash.

Once we saw it empty up, we started putting our things like laptops, books and important papers in there. We started treating it like our office. Now the juices began to flow with our mind activating ideas for the room.

To our surprise, our girls gave us a trip to Hawaii for

Christmas in 2019. When they were youngsters, we would travel there the last two weeks of October, since their elementary school was on a modified schedule. While on this return trip after 15 years had passed, we enjoyed shopping in galleries and looking at the local artwork available. Since we had ideas for our new space, we really wanted to fill it with scenes we've always enjoyed in Hawaii.

By moving the beds in their old room, we now have space for our yoga mats, working, or creating and looking at the Hawaiian prints which really help us relax. After all, that's what we were looking to accomplish. Although we miss our girls, we wanted this space to help us recline and soften our minds. How lovely to look at those beautiful Hawaiian pictures and remind ourselves what our children gave us.

The time you take to declutter and organize is worth every minute. It is a bit sad as you begin to put their items away, but now you can put up images that represent your current state of mind. A great way to turn this from sad to inspirational is to see all the achievements they've accomplished and celebrate them every moment when you're in that unique space. It is important to notice all you've done as their parents and proclaim victory.

31

Reexamine Your Finances

Once the dust settled, we had a chance to sit down with our bills. Because we weren't heading out to one sporting event or another each weekend for our daughters, we had a chance to really examine what we were paying for each month. Use this sacred time to really lay out all your bills and budget to see where all the funds are going. Look through all the automatic withdrawals and see if they are still needed. Now it's time to find some extra money to put into that travel jar!

During children's middle school and high school years, there are many things that happen in a family's life. Some parents get laid off, some students need medical care, and some families experience divorce. In addition, there might be monthly withdrawals for their sports or other activities and not to mention the extra television apps.

They may have set up withdrawals with your account for the local YMCA. It is time to reexamine what your payments look like every month. It might be necessary to pull up a few bank statements to see all the automatic withdrawals. Also, it is time to look at your medical bills and make sure they have medical coverage that covers them if they study out of state. Let's see how to sort this out.

As you begin to scroll through your previous bank statements, be sure to call the bank representative to pull up all automatic withdrawals of any subscriptions. From their purchase of television apps to even magazine subscriptions, be sure to look over any withdrawals for workout programs that they have connected to their phone. It is time to cancel these unnecessary items.

They may put up a fuss, but simply remind them that they can purchase these themselves and have the automatic withdrawal taken from their own account. This usually brings a sneer. Parents can always remind their children that they can find a part time job near college in order to keep the subscriptions they like. In addition, this is a way to introduce them to the real world, the grownup world.

While our daughters were in high school, there were job layoffs with added credit card debt to help get through the humps. There was also a time when we both had two jobs each just to keep things moving forward. As they talked about going to college back East, new bills came to mind such as transportation costs and medical expenses in another state.

When you think you have found good insurance coverage for them and make the purchase, be sure to call multiple times, getting a different representative each time to know they will be covered. Be sure that what others said about the coverage is correct. We paid for one in Rhode Island and it turned out to be useless.

Before we had our children, we talked about how we were going to financially do this family thing. We agreed that I would be a stay-at-home mom for their first five years. It was discussed that by staying at home for those years it would hurt my chances of having a good job later. In order to cover college tuition, we made a deal that we would refinance our home in order to pay for any child rearing. Little did we know that our oldest would have a funny intestine that would lead to specialists and surgery?

This happened as her dad was laid off and as we used our home equity to cover these huge payments. Since we didn't have control over our daughter's health, it is wise to remember that anything can happen. Be sure to cover as many bases as you can, especially by creating a savings account to help with these surprises.

As your nest becomes empty, start this reexamination so you can have more funds in your wallet. It's important to become clear on all your funds. It's time to take control of the things you pay for and investigate every automatic withdrawal. Although some payments will end, others will begin. There are different costs like transportation, books, and meals.

Knowing exactly where your money is going is crucial. Once you know where every penny is going, it's easy to start saving and canceling subscriptions no longer needed. Being aware of where your money goes will help you prepare for surprises and get some well deserved sleep.

32

Time to Relax

Remember way back when your children were young and how you eyed your couch wanting to be relaxing on it? How about the memory of starting to look through a magazine only to be called away to solve someone's problem? Never fear, your time is here.

It is time to go throughout the house grabbing all the magazines you put aside and form a pile. Maybe look through the pantry locating your favorite boxes of tea. Put all the couch pillows in your favorite spots and lounge.

Open your favorite magazines and start flipping through. After all the disturbances while raising your kids, it is finally time to sit still and read up on your favorite people, new recipes, or a new theory of living. No longer will you be alerted to a problem where you have to jump up like a firefighter going to the pole and getting in the fire truck. It is time to recall how to be selfish, lick your finger, and start turning those pages.

If your other self starts making excuses to why you shouldn't be doing this, start a list of your own reasons why you should. There were years of breast or bottle feeding not to mention how many diapers you changed. Be sure to think of all the times you were in a deep sleep only to have to jump out of bed to respond to their cries. Reminisce how each morning you woke them up, made breakfast, and ushered them to the car trying not to be late. Call to mind the nights where you were on boogie monster duty or comforted a tummy ache. Think of the numerous times you sat in your car driving them to school, work, a friend's house, a play date, or a birthday party. Try not to relive all the fights you had with your children, however bring to mind all the struggles you lived through too.

Last, look back at all the early morning breakfast sandwiches and lunches you made on a weekend with the long drives taking them to their sporting events. You earned your sessions on the couch.

Relaxing is a healthy choice. It helps to lower your blood pressure, brings homeopathic relief to a headache, and is a great way to rest your weary toes. This is the time of life where you focus on you and your health. Let yourself know that it isn't selfish to take care of you.

Since this is a new phase of your life, there's no reason why you need to be working every second. Put you as priority one. After doing all the hard parts of raising a child, it's time to kick back and rest. There's nothing better than taking deep breaths in and out knowing that you accomplished the hardest job on earth, being a parent.

For six years straight, we were traveling to Los Angeles, Las Vegas, and Phoenix for volleyball tournaments and local freeways for swim meets and water polo events. The weekends were filled with those functions leaving the last few hours on Sunday evenings to get ready to do it all over again. You've earned the right to go around your house to collect all the magazines you put away for another time. That time is now. Spend time putting them in date order and dive in. Enjoy each pillow and be sure to elevate those feet. They've been everywhere for a long time, so they are in need of some pampering too.

Maybe relaxing comes in the way of a cup of tea and simply breathing. Turn the kettle on, pick a favorite bag and pull out your cherished mug. Head to the couch that isn't being taken up by your teenage children, and get comfortable. It might hit the spot to listen to soothing music or watch a beloved film. In any case, reacquaint yourself with your couch and put your feet up. Take advantage of this special time. Remind your brain of what you deserve and what you worked so hard for.

As you notice the nest is quieter, take advantage of this and indulge. Recognize all the goals you accomplished and all the dreams you helped come true. Reacquaint yourself to your couch, bust open your magazines, sip your tea, and breathe in all the goodness you deserve.

33

Embrace Your New Schedule

Becoming an Empty Nester means it's time to do things differently. Parents are accustomed to a schedule which usually requires rushing from place to place. As you are in this new phase of life, it's time to put an end to that past schedule and start embracing your new schedule by filling your days with fun and relaxation.

Those days of doing the same thing and running yourself ragged are in the past. It's time to fill your calendar with important things that matter to you. Start filling in lunch dates with friends, hair and nail appointments, and coffee with an old acquaintance. Be sure to spread them out giving you time to relax and breathe.

Going from burning up each minute to having some time to spare can be a weird feeling at first. Before when your nest was buzzing and each day had its specific events, you marched through it every week. Once you stop and listen, you'll see the flow of time open up on your calendar.

As you think of all the fun times you can schedule, make sure to leave time for just hanging out and relaxing. Having time to finally breathe and be present will do your heart good. Take advantage of no longer having to cart everyone around and create meals for them. When you sit in your new found moments, think of the happenings that are fun and calming. Give your heart breathing room and schedule fun, but also time for rest.

I recall sitting in my first quiet moments. At first, the silence was strange and then my eyes went right to the dust and walls thrashed with marks. What happened was the second thought that came to me. Be sure not to fill your schedule with all the to-do items. However, create a list of things to fix, clean, or repaint down the line.

As you start filling in your calendar, schedule only a few of these to-do chores. Better yet, spread out the work. If you are looking at repainting, spend one weekend cleaning the area and purchasing the paint and equipment. Then schedule the actual painting for another time. There's absolutely no reason why you can't take it slow and easy.

My schedule used to consist of leaving work, picking up the kids, going back out to tutor, and then returning home to cook meals and then cart them to their sports practices. After late pickups, they ate their dinner and I remember seeing their lights on late while they did assignments for school.

Now, my schedule is for me. I started filling my days every other week meeting up with a friend for popcorn and a coffee. We would catch up, tell the latest stories, and laugh. That was the best part of filling my own schedule. I made sure my calendar was filled with relaxing and fun times. Not to waste gas, I would stop off and pick up items I needed to work on the house. Little by little I would gather what I needed to fix or paint my home and more importantly I did it at my pace. This may seem like something so small, but it will create a huge smile on your face. Once you practice filling your time the way you want, you'll see that it is a great way to stay healthy and stress free.

As your kids are off on their own, your mind thinks of them often at the beginning. However, as you practice being the priority in your life, you become calmer and happier. Your children will see your happiness and it will help them move through their homesickness too. Even though they are grown, they still watch and do what you do. No longer will you be the mom rushing around. You've stepped into the stage of eating popcorn, enjoying a coffee with a friend and having some good belly laughs.

34

Putting Off Big Decisions

The kids are gone, but the way you are handling this in your heart and mind has a big impact on your decision making. Be sure to hold off on any big decisions in your life. Maybe you're finally thinking of moving because you want a new life or you finally want to put yourself first. Take a moment to stop, breathe and think about your next step.

There's absolutely nothing wrong with having new dreams of buying a new house or car, or starting a new business. These are all wonderful ideas; however research finds that we should hold off on large decision making until we find out how we really feel.

Since becoming empty nesters can come with some anxiety, researchers suggest that we move cautiously during this time. In The Journal of Neuroscience, we learn that anxiety works to disengage the part of the brain that is essential for making good decisions. Scientists at the University of Pittsburgh have found out how the pre-frontal cortex can take charge of our thoughts when under duress. Knowing this, we might want to create a third choice for our decision which is to let it sit for a while and return to it at another time.

Based on research where they study people who are in a stressful stage, men become bigger risk takers when they have a big decision in front of them while women become more conservative. If we can take a longer time to think and mull over a big decision, it will give us time to make a good decision that fits our lifestyle and not one that is merely in our imagination.

There is absolutely no reason not to have great ideas pop into our mind. The question is how to maneuver through them. As we should with any big decision, we can do research and plot our moves within the coming months. By collecting our personal data and creating a pros and cons sheet, we can determine if the idea is something to work on further and when it should happen.

I remember going to Open Houses to see what was out there and what the price of new homes were in my neighborhood. When visiting staged homes, I got great ideas to freshen up my own. After looking at the prices of a new mortgage along with our monthly income, it helped us see that moving at that time wasn't the answer.

In fact, it would only increase our stress levels. However, in divine timing, going to these open houses gave us some wonderful ideas. Some great ideas included new wood flooring and contemporary furniture to help give us that change we were looking for in our new stage of life. So if there is a swift idea to buy a new luxury car, or buy a new house and sell your old, do the research and take your time on making this big decision.

As we live in our new empty-nest stage, we see the emotional stress that comes along with it. By weighing options, planning, and looking at the logical side of the idea, we give our brain time to sort through the information as well as our feelings on the matter. When we allow ourselves time to think about the idea, it lets us live with the idea and see how it fits first.

35

Understanding Your Adult Children

One of the best parts of being a mom is witnessing the maturity of your child. It feels like doing a swan dive into all the positive quotes you can find. "Hanging out with your adult children is like visiting the most beautiful and precious parts of your life." And, "Happiness is when you realize your children have turned out to be good people." These are just some of the beautiful sentiments you'll find. Be sure to hold onto these wonderful thoughts and prepare your mind for the day they want to discuss something from their past that has always bothered them.

Being with your adult children is a new world that can be rewarding or like walking on eggshells. If the tide turns and you find yourself clutching your heart wondering what has made everything sour, keep in mind that it is just another stage in life that they are going through.

We knew from the very beginning that children move in and out of stages at rocket speed. Just as we'd finally understand one stage, they'd be moving on to the next. Recall the adjustments you had to make with your heart and mind. Going through a new stage with an adult child is the same. Now there are new circumstances that are more adult in nature, but that could also have a hint of immaturity. Like the past, look for the problem using eyes of love and calm the heart to consider a solution.

The phone call ended and the harsh words still swirled around. Although it feels heavy, reminiscing about past stages our children went through can pop into our minds. Since moms have gone through so many of these stages with them, we know how to keep the personal to one side and turn to the evidence of what is actually happening in this new stage of life. It may feel like a dagger through the heart as your brain starts asking the old question, "After all the love I gave, how can he say those things to me?"

When they let out the problem, be ready to clutch your pearls. It will feel like the wind was knocked out of you and you need to learn how to breathe again, but go to your safe space of being a loving mom. We know how many times we ventured there to keep the peace and to help hold ourselves together. This is just another moment where we practice counting to ten the way we did as they sprawled around on the floor having their temper tantrum. We acknowledge their hurt, we notice our part in it, we offer a heartfelt apology, and we learn from the situation at hand.

My best advice is to look into articles or books that reveal the pain that a parent will feel and how to maneuver through this stage before it occurs. There are coaches for helping parents with their adult child relationships as well as videos online that can help. Because we saw them off to college or into their new apartment, it doesn't mean our lessons with them are over.

We also need to remember that they have their own opinions, likes, and wants. It is important to offer our opinions only when asked. Listening may be the real key here. By listening, we are letting our adult children be heard. Let them know you have ideas, but only offer them if they ask for them.

We must remember that our children are allowed to have their own ideas and opinions. When I am listening to one of my children share something they're going through, I make sure to listen and only offer my two cents when asked. I might even ask if they want to hear my idea by asking, "I have an idea that might help with the topic we discussed." I've also offered a text that stated, "I have some ideas about the subject we talked about. Do you want to hear them?" By offering your opinion in that manner, it lets them decline in an easy way. As I asked this to one daughter, her reply was thanks, but not right now. It helps keep me in my boundaries while also acknowledging hers.

After the initial pain of hearing their side of the problem they had with you, remind yourself this is a new stage. Recall the steps you took in the past in order to bring about a solution. It takes love and understanding. We need to remember that we didn't lash out at them when they tumbled off their bike when they were first learning to ride.

Although they yelled out in anger and frustration, we need to remember that this is the same case. At this age, we need to realize they are flexing their adult muscles, finding their way, and figuring out their own independence.

Once they learned to ride that bike, they smiled from ear to ear as you grinned in return for their success. We need to do the same here. Giving understanding and mercy is part of step one along with counting to ten as needed. Since I always remember them as toddlers, I had to remind my brain to focus on who they are now. Giving them time to hash out their problem will be needed along with the thought that this too will pass.

PART FOUR

Working On You

36

Take Care of You – Book Those Doctor Appointments

It is said that we must take care of ourself because no one else will. With our nest empty, it gives parents more time to be first. With some parents traveling with their kids to their sporting events for the past four years, all that fast food may be catching up. Rushing here and there, we might not have been taking good care of our body the way we should have. Although many don't like to go to the doctor or dentist, it is a good time to think about having your check-ups done. Because we've been there for our children, it's time to focus on ourselves and make our dentist and doctor appointments.

Some feel anxiety when they think of going to the dentist or the doctor. However, think back to how you made sure your children had their teeth cleaned and had physicals for school and their sports teams.

Now it's your turn. Take it slow when you start off. Remember, your gum health is linked to your heart. If you haven't been to the dentist in awhile, ask a friend who they use and go in for a cleaning. They most likely will do x-rays to look for decay, but simply hold off on anything major. Some new dentists like to promote gum cleaning which can result in a lot of money and isn't always necessary. Be sure to have a regular check up and then discuss your outcome with your spouse or a friend. They'll help you move forward.

Every year you made sure your child had their check-ups and inoculations. Their health was number one on your list. It's time to put yourself there. If you haven't seen your doctor except when ill, it is time to get your numbers weight, blood pressure, and cholesterol. These numbers will determine whether to change your diet, get more exercise or both. Because these numbers affect your overall health, step up and have them checked. After all your work raising your children, be sure your body is ready for their second half of your life.

Since our children decided to go back East for college, it added a bit of stress. While at a doctor appointment for a sinus infection, my husband saw how his blood pressure had increased. After thinking about it, he knew his drink every night and not exercising were a big reason for the increase. As I went to the doctor for the same thing, I saw how much weight I gained and realized it was time to get back in shape. By eliminating his drink to only Fridays and both of us beginning to walk every day, we saw a significant drop in his blood pressure and my weight.

While our girls were home and doing their sports, we were eating late and not always eating healthy. After playing her volleyball tournaments my younger daughter was ready for a burger, however, as only spectators we were indulging also. We decided to enjoy grilled chicken and meat with grilled veggies at home and avoid heavy carbs and only indulge those choices for once a week when out.

As my husband got home from work, we would catch up on each other's day with a walk. It becomes a huge realization that your children are out in the world and starting their life. Soon they will marry and have children. If you think the first 18 years flew by, get ready. It really starts picking up speed.

Since you worked so hard on taking care of your children all those years, it's time to do the same for you. No one likes going to the doctor or dentist, but once you go, you'll know what to work on next. It's a great feeling when you start to make changes that help your health.

By making small changes in your eating and exercise, you'll become stronger and happier. Next change the walks to a bike ride or hike. With you in charge of your schedule, select all the fun activities that put a smile on your face. Can you imagine the looks on their faces when your kids come home for that first visit home from college?

37

Get to Know You through Meditation

What a perfect time to start working on You! We've all heard it before as we looked through magazines, viewed our email, or scrolled through Facebook. Now we're at that stage where we finally have time to focus on meditation and find out which ones are best for us.

As I read an article online from the website Healthline, I reviewed the different kinds of meditation that are available to try. My opinion when starting is to simply sit quietly with or without soothing music and breathe. Some meditations have you focus on your breath, a phrase, your thoughts or a combination of all of those. After sitting and focusing on the area that makes you most comfortable, take time to read about the six types of meditation and pick the ones that you enjoy.

Remember, this is a time to get to know yourself better, but you also want to select things that bring you comfort and joy. Six meditations that Healthline reviewed were mindfulness, movement, mantra, spiritual, focused, and transcendental. Mindfulness, mantra, and spiritual meditations come from their Eastern teachings and some use candles or essential oils.

Mindfulness meditation is popular in the West, where you look at your thoughts and their patterns, as well as transcendental meditation which is more customizable than mantra-based and has more scientific studies. One is for those who seek silence and go deeper in their spiritual growth where others use movement or phrases to concentrate on. Depending on what you are looking to accomplish, any of these will help you open up in the practice that fits you best.

With your new found time, schedule your meditation time. Simply start out slowly and build. This can simply be sitting and living in the moment. It's a way of grounding yourself. Sit and breathe a few times in silence and with soothing soundscape music to determine if you enjoy meditating with or without music.

Make time to read up on the six types of meditation and try each one. Look online for help and meditation sessions. Remember to keep it fun and soothing. It shouldn't be rushed or pushed. You decide which one you enjoy best. At first, you may feel uneasy because it's a new process of slowing your mind.

Stick with it to give it time, but don't force it to the point of becoming frustrated. Enjoy the perks that come along with meditating such as lower blood pressure, reduced anxiety and depression, and improvement in sleep. As you introduce your mind to this new concept, give yourself permission to relax and learn.

Whenever I heard the words meditation or yoga, I thought you had to be "with it" in order to do them. I found that just by starting meditation, it became my best friend next to my relaxing bike rides. I remember starting from a video online where someone walked me through. It was the mindfulness meditation where I practiced letting my thoughts come up and letting them go by without reliving them.

Once I worked on letting my thoughts go by, it helped me understand the flow and how to work through all those crazy thoughts coming. More importantly, it made me understand that there is no correct way to meditate. It is me sitting with my thoughts by focusing on my breathing or a phrase and relaxing.

Now that I had a better understanding, I signed up for a free 21 day meditation program that I came across online. I would do these when I got home from work or sometimes in my car during my lunch break. These meditations are more transcendental in type where you focus on a phrase of the day based on the subject of the day like hope or forgiveness.

After I started feeling more confident and comfortable, I tried other types online with other masters of spirituality like Wayne Dyer. I tried one of his mantra meditations, but it wasn't something I enjoyed, although I love all his books and videos. By this time, it struck me to select and do only the ones I appreciate.

Similar to Irene Cara, I was hearing myself sing the phrase from her song, "Oh, What a Feeling!" It is probably the best feeling in the world for your body and mind. Meditating is one of my favorite things to do and it costs nothing but your time.

My body feels better and my mind seems to work even better. Like anything, it has to be practiced daily. There are times when I feel lousy and wonder why my thoughts are so negative. That is usually when I see that I have replaced my meditation time with something else. In order to keep it on your slate, have your phone alarm scheduled and set up to remind you daily.

This is a great time to use technology for good, so grab your phone, click on the clock and set your meditation time right now. Start slow and build. Enjoy relaxing your mind and seeing the world in a better body.

38

Work on Your Spiritual Path

Most of us don't realize our spiritual path even when we're on it. Once we see it, we want the whole world to see it through our eyes. Considering that thought, we must remember it is a very personal experience. We all seek that positive and loving space, but fall off our course, and have to learn how to get back on track.

Sometimes raising a family or work pushes us off that path we were following, so it's up to us to get back on. Don't get me wrong, as a mother, our spiritual path is right there every step of the way helping us make choices and pressing through the hard times.

However, all the details that we tend to have start weaving us on and off our path. Now that our kids are doing their thing, we are able to put our full attention on our path and start filling it with positive energy.

As we live in our new world without our children around, we find empty space to fill. This is the perfect time to fill it with new and healthy ways to help us get back on track. Find a quiet place and contemplate the routines you were doing or always wanted to do when you were reaching for your higher self. You may recall finding time here and there to meditate or even times when you read books by healers that helped, but now you have the time to look even deeper.

Mothers realize they were on their spiritual path the whole time. Every element of raising their children included their spiritual practices. From infant to high school age, we were finding moments within our day to stay on our path. In light of our small amount of time, we found moments to stay positive. Nowadays, we can put more time into our practices and continue down our unique paths.

As one tries to find their spiritual path, it is evident that we're already on it. We took different forks on the road as we traveled. When our job of raising our children shifts and changes, so does our focus and allotted time.

While we were moving through the many stages of motherhood, we implemented the practices we learned. At the time of rocking our child, we practiced meditation but only in a different form. In the course of teaching our little ones the do's and don'ts of eating and walking, we were practicing our breathing methods. As our children grew and had upsets, we practiced our prayers even while we were driving to the grocery store or even a sporting event.

During all these new jobs of ours, we kept up our practices; we just didn't look at them that way. From praying to breathing, we used what we learned up to that point. At this point, since our chickadees have left the nest, we can now start to dig further and deeper into our own spirituality and how we want to practice that.

Think back to the different ways you found your peace. It may have included different forms of meditation, yoga, reading and listening to your favorite healers, and simply walking while visualizing positive aspects. Despite all the time that has passed, start researching those you knew from the past. There are also new healers out there as well. Choose someone you feel aligns with your core values and beliefs. They will help you get back on this reignited path or can help you take your very first steps.

Begin to read the books from the past that helped like, The Four Agreements. As you walk for exercise, listen to Wayne Dyer and new healers such as Matt Kahn and Kyle Cease. Find the old goodies and include the new ones by watching their videos or listening to their podcasts.

Since my running days became my walking days, I would use the time to practice thinking positive thoughts. As soon as a negative thought came in, I'd practice thanking it for showing up, but would turn my mind to something positive. From seeing the beauty in a flower, to simply breathing in and out, I looked for the good in everything.

It takes time, but as you practice these more and more, your mind becomes trained. These times helped me get into my flow by asking what I can do to help someone. Because I took the focus off me and my problems, I was shown how to help others. Writing on my blog and writing my books took off. I was nudged and whispered to share everything I healed from because there were others out there who needed to heal as well.

With all your new time to clean up and renovate your space, find a spiritual leader who speaks to you and listen to their speaking engagements. While I would work in the kitchen doing dishes and cooking, I would listen to Matt Kahn and Kyle Cease. They would help me through things that were going on in my life that I pushed off in order to raise my kids, but were now coming back because they needed to be healed.

During this time when I felt open, it was the perfect time for me to listen to ways to approach my heartache and find a positive outlook. In order to stay away from insomnia, I would read books like The Seat of the Soul by Gary Zukav to Everything is Here to Help You by Matt Kahn. Instead of reading, listening to a meditation as you drift off to sleep may help as well.

With your new time, fill it with those who can help you on your spiritual path. They will help you surrender your old habits and allow you to let your true feelings come through.

Reintroduce all the things you enjoyed before, and you'll notice you were never lost while on your path. As you read and listen to your new spiritual friends, you will find that wonderful flow you found every now and then as you helped your little ones through the tough times of life.

Don't be surprised if at some point your children ask you who it was that you listened to while you cooked and they were doing their homework. What a perfect time to share your journey as they start down their own spiritual path.

39

Get Back in Shape

Many times over the years, I've heard groans and moans come out of my own body whenever I spoke about getting back in shape. That time usually started at the end of December as I got ready for my New Year's resolution. As I've learned to outgrow that social convention, it did take a few years to grasp the lesson.

Because we parents put so much of our time into raising our kids, we probably neglected this area of health. Now that we are finding more time in our schedules for us, it's time to replace raising kids with getting back into shape. However, there is no need to groan anymore. This time of getting back in shape only includes the activities we love.

Whether we're early birds or love staying up late, determine what time of day you would enjoy doing these fun activities. The best thing about getting back in shape now is that you're in charge of what you do and when you do it. Include a friend or spouse to make it more enjoyable. Even if you can only think of a few things to do, just simply get started. Go easy on yourself and remind yourself to have fun.

Getting back in shape simply means moving your body and mind more. As we age, we find that many areas of our body begin to ache. By slowly beginning to move more, we can eliminate some of that pain.

If we maintain some kind of active lifestyle, we can live longer. Dr Saint-Maurice of the National Cancer Institute in the US says, "If you maintain an active lifestyle and participate in some sort of exercise over the window time of youth to middle age, you can reduce your risk of dying of cancer." He also added, "If you are not active and you get to your 40's -50's and you decide to become active, you can still enjoy a lot of those benefits."

Getting in shape is not only stretching the body, but also the mind. Not only moving your body, but engaging your mind in meditation can help get you back in shape. By meditating, you can help reduce stress and feel happier. The combination of a healthy body and mind can make us unstoppable.

Thinking back to my childhood, I always loved riding my bike, swimming and floating in a pool, hiking on easy trails, and walking on the shore of an ocean or lake. I looked at the areas closest to my home to start getting in shape outdoors. Simply walking was the first thing I did. I heard you can literally walk off weight and stress just by taking one step after another.

Sometimes our days can be filled with so much negativity. I added the idea of only thinking of positive thoughts. As soon as I caught myself drifting off to negative thoughts, I used the flowers and birds right in front of me to become positive again. Because it became a habit, I enjoyed my walks more and more. It became a safe space to stay positive in a world of craziness.

I also turned it into a learning experience; I'd take pictures of different plants and flowers and look them up online. Some I later even planted in my own yard. Creating a space where you can exercise and stay in your happiness can definitely contribute to getting your body and mind back into shape.

Some ride bikes for miles on rural roads or trails. I simply enjoy biking in my neighborhood and the large parking lot of my condominium complex. I was sure to select times when there would be less traffic and ventured out. Sometimes going out for a ride lasting 15-20 minutes was fun for me.

In addition to small bike rides, I began doing easy swimming and floating in a pool float. Although I was on a swim team as a youngster, I keep the laps easy and stop when I become tired. Remembering that I'm not training for the Olympics takes the stress off.

After the laps, I reward myself with some floating time. As I push off the pool's edge, I can create spins and waves. This is a great time to meditate. I'll either practice calling my angels to help with my writing or simply send love and light to those around me.

If you are willing to start slowly and select only the activities that mean something to you, you'll find yourself more fit both in your body and mind. Instead of forcing yourself through a workout that you find too hard, pick activities that are fun and bring you joy. In time, you'll see that the simple exercises and meditations help you become healthier and happier. You'll not only become fit but you'll find your smile and tranquility in the process.

40

Eating and Drinking Healthy Foods That Taste Good

One of the first things I noticed in this new empty nest stage was how the evening slowed down instead of ramping up when it came to dinner time. I wasn't rushing to accommodate everyone's different eating schedule. In addition, we were no longer living on quick takeout pizza. There were no scrambled feelings which left me time to think of and plan nutritious meals that I actually liked.

Because we make sacrifices on the grocery list to make others happy, we forget how much we love a certain food. Once you're in this sweet space of preparing what you love to eat, a whole new world opens up. Like I stated back in Chapter 22, I started buying the crunchy peanut butter and loving every minute of it. It really is all about the little things.

As a working mom and chauffeur, I had the responsibility of leaving work and then driving to pick up the girls at their high school, drop them off at home, and then rush off for tutoring. When I got home, it was time to whip up dinner for one child doing homework before traveling to volleyball practice. The other child who swam and played water polo couldn't eat until she was finished swimming. My husband ate when he got home from work which was always at a different time.

It's amazing how the world seems to open up when it comes to dinner time as an empty nester. As we began actually grocery shopping together, we started realizing that we could make all our favorite meals. More than that, we were seeing the world from a different angle. We could actually go out for a quick bite at old favorite places and new eateries near us on occasion.

While I think back to those tough times of limited funds for groceries with no extra money to eat out, I remember the time we traveled to one of our daughter's volleyball tournaments in Las Vegas. Because it was important to make a showing at these tournaments since many college recruiters attended, we had to make it all work on our budget.

At home, I prepared many teriyaki bowls that my daughter could heat up in our low-budget hotel room. We brought bagels with cream cheese and cut up fruit in a large bowl. Even though these items were available at the tournaments, we were able to save a lot of money by bringing them ourselves.

I remember as we were unloading bags late one night into our hotel room after a long drive, the large bowl of the cut cantaloupe spilled. My daughter's face looked so horrified and scared. Right away we tried to save the good pieces. She knew our budget and looked sad. I told her not to worry and we could find a grocery store in the area and get more.

On the last evening in Las Vegas at her tournament, we always sacrificed our money for her to partake in a buffet that the team players enjoyed together. As parents, we know how to eat a banana for dinner. Thinking back to those tight-walleted moments, I can see how we all had to sacrifice and how we made it work in those days.

Those were definitely great times to recall and certainly moments of lessons learned. I like to think that these memories helped shape both parent and child alike. Now in this new stage, we're excited to enjoy cuisine that we missed.

Not much of a cook? Today is a great time to live if that's the case. With all the cooking shows and videos available, what a great time to be alive! There are also wonderful new companies that put together meals along with step by step instructions. My daughter and her husband ordered meals from one of these and absolutely loved it. It not only had great instructions, but it was a way for them to purchase groceries and make the meal themselves.

What about a recipe you love but never had the time to make because you were venturing off to sporting events? My friend's homemade stew recipe was finally something I had time to make. While at her home during one of the college drop off years, she walked me through her recipe. Now I have time to make it and think back on that great day when she taught me.

Since we're starting to take care of ourselves by getting back to the doctor to be sure our numbers are in the safe zones, we can start taking short drives to look around and seek out new places that offer delicious authentic food that will help keep us healthy. By doing this, we can find places that offer vegetables and fruits to our liking. What a great time to try other ethnic foods we always wanted to taste.

While enjoying these new eateries or fine meals at home, what a wonderful time to see how far you've come and where you are today. Seeing the path you came from can be a comfort and reminder to how much growth has taken place in your life. Taking the time to notice where you came from and where you are now is huge. Smile as you take in new ways to eat and as you try new foods. Remind yourself that you deserve this time.

41

Spend Some Money on your New Look

As we raise our children, we usually put all our resources into them. When they finally leave the nest, we have time to look around and notice that we are in need of a new wardrobe. While we go through our closet, we realize how old some of our pieces of clothing are on those hangers. Your eyes may even pop out of your head when you recall wearing something a decade ago. Yes, that's the moment you decide to start finding bags to fold up the old for a thrift shop or simply throw away some garments and start looking for some new fresh ones.

Time certainly flies when we're having fun. Even though we feel young we don't want to make the mistake of purchasing clothing out of our age group, nor do we want to wear clothing that old ladies back in your childhood wore. Things are different and it's time to pick what we like and make sure it is affordable and comfortable.

It might be fun to hit a bookstore with a coffee shop next door and finger through some magazines to spot that perfect top and slacks. Maybe make your favorite tea or coffee at home and enjoy going online to find what's out there in today's fashion. How exciting to find a sale going on with one of your favorite brands or one of your favorite stores. If the price of some apparel doesn't seem to fit your current budget, start putting aside a little each paycheck to cover the cost. As you save, you have time to fill your online shopping cart.

When my girls were studying back East, I was lucky enough to have a husband who worked for a closet company. After my new closet with drawers was installed, I started collecting a few items here and there. I asked a few friends which online stores they enjoyed ordering from and started shopping when I found a few moments.

I recall a morning when I was headed to work and sitting at a red light. I looked down and realized everything I was wearing was brand new. Such an overwhelming feeling of gratitude came over me. I could remember having to wear the same two pairs of pants when I was a reading teacher in the past. Now I was headed to a new school to teach in special education wearing clothes that fit great and made me feel confident and amazing.

After all the sacrifices you made for your children, this is the time to finally put YOU first. Ask your friends where they might shop. Someone you know might have a style you love, so be sure to find out where they shop and have fun making you a priority.

It may feel weird because every bit of extra money went towards their AP exams, sports, or school events. As your children are experiencing the adult world, it is time to reacquaint yourself to the new world around you.

Remind yourself how worthy you are to receive these new clothes. Feel the gratitude of your new purchases and the thankfulness for being able to wear the new clothing. Think back to the many times you put an item back on the rack as you raised your children. Smile and enjoy the great pleasure of hanging your new apparel and seeing your smile in the mirror as you get dressed in the morning.

42

Find Your Passion and Turn it into Your Job

I don't know about you, but I always had the passion to write. However, as my career changed from Marketing and Sales to a stay-at-home mom, I was left with no extra time to pursue my parenting book or blogs. Keeping my mind on the elementary room-mom gig for two children lasting eight years only left me minimal time for self-care and most of that was only rebuilding my energy and keeping a peaceful mind to deal with those little humans.

As the kids moved from elementary to middle school grades, I was consumed with my reading teacher job along with being a taxi driver and chef for two scholar athletes. I was smart to occasionally jot down ideas for chapters to research how children's brains grow. Once they were scheduling all our weekends with their sporting tournaments on travel teams, I made sure to learn the ropes and see all the opportunities that were out there for scholar athletes in college.

Now that the house is empty, start thinking about all those ideas you had while you were raising your little pumpkins. (Hence writing this bit in October) Maybe you wanted to learn a craft, look into cooking or baking, or hike the PCT the way you always dreamt? Start filling your time with courses or time to venture off toward your passion.

What's been mulling around in your head? I've always had the thought and idea of writing a parenting book based on the scholar athlete girls I received. Because I stayed within reach of my passion for writing, I was able to use my new free time to begin learning how to write a book and start online courses to learn as much as possible.

Be sure to share your ideas during your calls and video chats with your college student. This not only helps you learn through your new passion, but helps to switch gears from parent to entrepreneur. Think of all the fun and/or extra money this may bring in.

There will most definitely be a cost for your new found adventure, but remind yourself that it can all be achieved through the funds from having a smaller grocery bill and no monthly sports fees. Even if you need to work a few extra hours or take on an extra income job like tutoring or babysitting, it will be well worth it.

With weekends to yourself, plan a girls' appetizer night with neighbors, who have small businesses or jobs that can help answer questions. For the cost of some food and drinks, you can ask great questions and receive informative ideas.

I did just that with my neighbor friends. I picked a local place & had my husband chauffeur us. Since they're 15 years younger, I asked questions about social media. My questions were mostly on Instagram since that was my new social media. With friends from Twitter, I was conquering how to meet other writers and groups that may help with the marketing of my book. They were helpful with hashtags, reels, and when to use them.

Letting your true passion out adds to your positive well-being. Because you are living in your element and have your thoughts focused, your whole self is breathing happier. Not only am I helping myself, but hopefully my parenting book will help other moms and parents raise their kids and help them through the college process world. Your smile will be seen by others to help ignite their passion or to help pull them into their light. Either way, you are helping to make the world a happier place.

43

Listen to Your Soul

Remember those hints from your gut and ways you were guided as you raised your children? This is a great time to go back to using that strategy you touted around with you back then. In order to achieve this, meditation might be a great strategy here as well as getting quiet to listen to your soul and notice signs.

Since we have more time in our schedule as an empty nester, we should start filling it with things that will add a positive vibe to our day. One way to get back to listening to your soul is to meditate daily. It is a way of simply practicing the important art form of patience and noticing the 'now'. Another way we were guided was by watching for the synchronizations happening around us. By noticing and following those signs like a popcorn path, we found answers to problems or things that were troubling us.

We all remember those days of counting to ten while we were bringing our stress level down after a child's behavior elevated it. Meditation is a way of attaining that quiet space where we allow all the old feelings and ideas to release from us, so we can let in the amazing. When we take time everyday to sit quietly or with soothing music, we are not only helping our heart health, but our emotional health as well.

Other times where we noticed how things were all adding up, we followed the signs that helped us with a struggle. One time I received a text from a family member that wasn't so kind. At that moment, I remembered I had a meditation call scheduled. Even though I wasn't in the right frame of mind, I saw how this was actually the perfect timing. By listening to the meditation call, I was able to bring myself to a calm point where I didn't want to lash out at the text received. In the meantime, I came across a video that matched up with exactly what was happening to me. I made time to watch and listen and saw how phenomenal it was that these moments came to me at the time I really needed them.

My guru says these things always come to us when we need them the most. When we're open, signs will come because we simply ask for help. If we think about it, we are always guided by those special people who have gone on before us and even those wonderful angels looking over our lives. In the past, we might remember how great ideas quickly came to us in our time of need. Through meditation and looking for the signs, we live in that positive and productive space.

There was a time when I was a stay at home mom and bills were piling up, so I knew I needed to find a part time job. I remember being guided out of bed late one night, and being pulled to find the want ads section of the newspaper, (this was the 90's) and noticing a part time job at a local car dealership. It was only a short drive from my home, so I called the next day. It turned out that they needed someone to answer phones on two evenings during the week and on weekends. For six months I enjoyed my time conversing with adults on the weekends and found time to do my teaching credential studies during the two evening times. All in all, because I followed my heart and the signs, my angels helped guide me to extra money to help alleviate my problem.

Not only will you notice a decrease in your blood pressure as you fit meditation into your life, but your smile will find its way back on your face. When we take time to simply sit and breathe, we are allowing our body to let go of bad emotions. As we let thoughts come up to be seen but not wrestled with, we are learning how to let go of what no longer serves us. By being open to the signs brought to our mind, we can be helped in any problem.

If you are not familiar with meditation, simply look up online the different types and start the kind that fits for you. With today's technology, there are some on YouTube or certain apps for meditation that can point you in the right direction. Enjoy noticing how much calmer you become. When it comes to noticing your signs, get quiet and slow your breath. As you ask for help, be prepared to notice your signs show up and begin to guide you. Since these strategies will put you in a better mindset, you may find yourself getting out more or trying new things. By simply putting a reminder on your phone to meditate, you will become stronger, healthier, and happier just because you decided to listen to your soul.

PART FIVE

Enjoying the Ride

44

Find Your Flow

Many people like to state that they are "in the flow". From athletes to writers, when they are in the flow, they feel the best they ever felt and love the positive feelings it emits. Famous swimmers always talk about being in their flow just like writers talk about starting to write in the morning and all of the sudden it's evening. However, some of us look at our own lives and wonder why we aren't achieving this flow or type of movement.

Some of us are observing others thinking, "How do they stay in the flow"? It takes me forever to get there. What is their secret? We see them talk about being in this wonderful state, but every time we try to step into it, it falls apart. What our problem can be is first having a negative mindset. Always living like Eeyore could be one important reason why we can't locate our flow. We don't want to live in a way where we are constantly fighting against things.

Another reason could be that we fight everything. Even though something doesn't match our feelings right away doesn't mean we have to go against it. When we bring on confusion or conflict, we are keeping ourselves from the flow. It's positive energy that moves us into being aware of our present time.

The psychology of flow is that it is a positive mental state while being present. As we become aware of the present moment, we can begin to step into our flow. Being in the flow is when one is focusing on the positive part of what they are doing. It is living in your presence as you're aligned and balanced from your positive thoughts to allowing another's way of thinking. By staying out of conflict or confusion doesn't mean we have less of those moments, we simply practice letting things go and letting them fall where they will.

Your flow will happen when there isn't fear. Once fear starts churning because there's confusion around, we need to meet this fear with calmness. Greet it and then watch it leave. This is the practice of being grounded.

When I'm motivated to do my writing, there is always the other side of the coin that wants me to do something else or the part of my mind that wants to come up with all these reasons why I can't. It might come to mind that I can't do this since I'm not in the right frame of mind. By whispering in my brain that what I'm writing is rubbish, I find myself wanting to stop and find something else to do. If I push through and keep on the writing trail, I find myself back in my flow. My mind might also try to tell me to do it the next day. When I thank those excuses for coming up, they usually leave which helps me find my flow again as well.

As I'm writing, something butts right in and says, "I wonder if your girls are trying to text you or maybe they sent a cute picture of their cat." The phone is the biggest reason for my falling out of the flow. Because it can really start to work on your imagination, the best thing to do is just turn it off and put it on the other side of the room. If you are waiting for an important message, simply put it farther away from your work area. When taking a peak during a break, remind yourself to only look for the important message. Just one peek can put you onto Facebook, your messages, and the next thing you know you are Googling birthday memes. Once the phone is out of sight and out of mind, we can discover our flow again.

The flow is a wonderful place to be and it takes practice to enter and remain there. When confusion comes, simply let go of that idea for the time being. Let yourself know that you will come back when in a more positive state. No fear or conflict can be present when wanting to get into the flow.

Meditation is a great strategy to get to the flow. Also, creating self-care moments like doing your toe nails, thumbing through a magazine, or laughing with friends helps put our mind in the positive space it needs to be for the flow. Practice moving away from conflict and avoiding confusion. When something becomes confusing, simply thank it for showing up and let it go for a while. In no time, you'll be in the flow and loving every moment of it.

45

Get Out of Your Rut

Am I in a rut? Does everyday seem the same and are you feeling unmotivated or feeling fear from the discomfort that comes along with change? Some might be thinking the answer is yes.

We're in a rut because sometimes the rut is a great place for us to hide from our true feelings and the happenings that are going on around us. In this rut, we can avoid venturing out into life since we are surrounded by what is familiar and comfortable. Whether our rut is dull or unproductive, this is a great time to pursue a new way of moving out of rut within your life.

If we sit and analyze our behaviors, we'll see we may no longer go out looking for a new restaurant or take the time to notice what new shops popped up since we've been carting our children to every athletic event or friend's house. It is time for us to change and move into our new stage of life with positivity.

I know better than anyone how nice it is to take the first few months of having our weekends to ourselves and enjoy every minute. All those water polo matches, swim meets, and volleyball tournaments almost every weekend for over 6 years had taken their toll. I recall saying out loud, "Wow, it is so nice to just sit and enjoy a cup of coffee on the weekend and relax!" It is absolutely the best feeling to look back and see your sacrifices in the past and what they accomplished. But now, take a breath and ask yourself the question, "Are you hiding in your rut?"

There is clearly a difference between enjoying your coffee on a weekend after several years in a row drinking it on the road and experiencing your rut of the same day never changing. You'll definitely feel unmotivated, unfulfilled, and bored. Because the source of your rut could be the absence of your children who left for college or moved out, it may be time to sit one weekend enjoying your coffee, but also thinking of different ways to come out of it.

Change is hard. When I was stuck in my rut, I literally started looking around at what was right in front of me in my world. As I needed to get a broken tooth fixed, I first smelled something amazing coming from a store in the same plaza. Since I had to have a follow up visit, I finally listened to those guides in my head and walked toward the wonderful smell. It turned out to be a Mediterranean store with food to go. We loved going to a family owned restaurant of this type miles away; I was thrilled that there was this one ten minutes from my house!

Another time we made a change out of our rut came with a simple parking pass. In our area near the beach, parking passes for the National State Parks on the coast waters are available for the year. What do you give a guy who has everything for Christmas? We decided to seek out a local state beach and use our pass. We hadn't been to that particular beach since we were first married. Once the kids were born, the price to park was too much for a stay-at-home mom, so I stopped going. Within miles from our house, we literally walked into the past using our parking pass. The tide was low, the sun was out, and the waves sounded like music to our ears. Being spontaneous really paid off.

Just from taking that one step toward that great smell and to a spot we visited years ago, we have opened up in our minds to a new place to eat our favorite Mediterranean food and a place to enjoy beauty while exercising with a little walk. I guarantee you will have a shift happen for you just by making a small behavioral change. It opens up your whole world. On one of our trips to another beach park, we saw a bowling alley we used to go to years ago. Can you guess what we're doing next?

46

You're Not Perfect and That's Okay

As we look back on any part of our life, we always seem to focus on the things we did bad or wrong. When you fall upon the old mementos and photos, this will prompt you to judge the past person you were. In this stage, the lesson is to practice moving the mind away from the negative thoughts and consistently replace them with positive ones. Even as we venture into this next stage, we do it at our own speed. If we falter, it is quite alright. It is the time in our life to remember that we're not perfect and that's ok!

In order to accomplish this, it takes two things: consistency and not being hard on one's self. Similar to Chapter 28, Get Out of the House and Explore, the trick is to be consistent with keeping your mindset on positive thinking.

The minute we notice that we're moving negative thoughts around in our mind that's when we need to look at it as something good. We need to be sure not to judge our thoughts. Instead, we can look at it as another moment to stay positive. Just like I've always told my children to be excited when they make a mistake, embrace the moment and practice thinking positively what can be learned from this mistake.

Sometimes this needs practice. As I would venture out on my walk, I had to immediately look at the thoughts in my head. So many times I would be thinking of missing my girls. I had to give myself rules on what to think about when on walks. Rule one was being vigil on what thoughts were in my head and rule two was being consistent with changing the negative ones to positive ones. I started creating a file in my head that had a handful of positive thoughts that I could turn to when the negative wanted to be in charge.

One positive thought is me sitting on a lounge chair in Maui watching whales breach. I have that picture on my refrigerator, and it always calms the savage beast. Another one was all the fun we would have the summers we spent with the kids in Maine at a camping resort. A third thought is remembering my volleyball daughter being moved around into different groups at a volleyball session of another club during try-outs. She eventually came over to us saying she was offered a spot on their national team. A last memory full of positivity was the weeks in August when I would travel back East with the girls to help move them into their pre-season and permanent dorms with my bestie.

Similar to how we learn to change our thoughts when we come home from work, we learn to turn off the thoughts of the day and happily engage in our family. Many of us have stressful jobs with problems throughout. Since we learned how to turn our minds from those negative thoughts, we need to do the same when we notice our thoughts taking us to our children leaving their nest.

It is essential to hesitate from beating up one's self when we notice we're bringing in sad thoughts of no kids at home. As you go for a walk with your spouse or alone, the conversation can turn to missing them, worrying about them, and creating a false story in our head. Instead of beating yourself up, simply smile, notice what you're doing and turn it around.

Gratitude is a good way to change your thoughts. By being grateful that they can attend college or start life on their own is always a great start. Realizing all the wonderful achievements our children accomplished can put us in a great frame of mind. Sitting present in the moment and gathering up all the hard work they achieved helps put us back on track. As I see young people wearing their team jerseys in stores, it brings a smile to my face remembering how much my girls struggled in their craft and how much it helped them mature. I notice the aspects that helped make them responsible individuals and it can always put a smile on my face.

From past research, it is said that we change a habit in 21 days. They estimate that a habit can be changed in approximately three weeks. In turn, we not only have to remember to change our thoughts from negative to positive, but also not be so hard on ourselves when it does happen. By practicing to be consistent with our mindset, we'll be smiling so much that others around us will be wondering what we're up to!

47

They Will Only Remember How You Made Them Feel

"I've learned that people will forget what you said, people will forget what you did, but people will never forget how you made them feel."

Maya Angelou

As an empty nester, there are many times that we wonder if everything we did for our kids is remembered. We think of our kids and wonder what they're doing as well as send our prayers. At the same time, they are thinking of us. All the little notes you left in their lunches, they might remember. All the little parties you made happen for them, they might think about. However, I've learned that all they really remember is how you made them feel.

When our children head off to college or work and live on their own, we look back on all the memories. Parents think back and notice how much they did for their children to make them feel happy. Some memories come from making a full haunted house for the many Halloween parties or recalling painting faces for their 7 year old birthday party. There were sacrifices of grocery money or other interests in order to make these events happen. Even if we spent a lot of time on the occasion, we moved through it all because of our emotions first.

"People decide emotionally and then justify it logically", states Brian Tracy, a speaker and author. He goes on to tell us that when it comes to our emotions, everything counts. Tracy reminds us that everything that happens in our life affects us emotionally in some way. In addition, he goes on to say that everything that affects us makes us happy or sad, motivated or unmotivated, loving or angry, fearful or confident.

As parents, we'll do anything possible to make our kids happy. We find out what their dreams are and then look into our wallet to see how much of it we can make happen. No matter the cost or hours put in, the best part is having them give us a big hug or smile as they thank us for making a dream come true.

Now when I'm sitting around the dinner table with my grown children, I love hearing all the memories they can recall. It's never about how much money we spent on something, but how much quality time they remember us putting into these special moments.

Every year since our oldest was 2 we had a Halloween party. At first it began very simply with a handful of friends who had children, some butcher paper covered tables with crayons, a few pumpkins and friendly ghost decorations, and a bucket of dunking apples filled with water. From age two until sophomore year in high school, we began adding creepy décor of scary clowns to frightful skeletons. A back room of our community house was transformed into the haunted scare room which our kids would scream their way through. My husband was always dressed up in something scary to help create the screams.

With one birthday in December and one in July, we used the seasons to create the celebration. Since living in CA in December is different from back East, we had options to go to a park at a young age, using the community house, or attending a Family Fun Center for pizza and games. For the birthday in July, there was always a pool party where they did line dancing and got to swing at a piñata.

No matter where we celebrated, it was always fun because we put our full focus on them and they felt it. One daughter was always so appreciative no matter what we did. They both helped create the celebration from helping to select the items to loading the car. The whole time I recall a smile on the one in the spotlight.

When Mother's Day approached during the pandemic, I knew funds were low as well as the ability to send an item was hindered. I asked for a simple letter with a few special memories.

I remembered being blown away by the things they recalled. I was in tears as I read how I made them feel happy and all the fun we had from flying a dollar store kite on the beach to having a cut day lunch at the local zoo and running into their previous teachers on a field trip. No one brought up how much something cost. All they remembered was how special I made them feel.

48

Send Out Your Love & Light

"I'm sending you love & light." Many around us may say this and we may very well use it in our daily lives.

Since our kids have left the nest, this is a time when we can use our energy to send love & light to those we know, to those who we haven't forgiven, to those we have forgiven but choose to stay away from, and to those we don't know who are struggling with a problem.

As I went to my community pool, I saw a woman who seemed to be enjoying the sun and I gave her a smile as I walked to an empty chair. When I was putting down my towel and bag full of sunscreen and water, I could hear her sniffle. Because I have allergies, I paid no mind. But as I started down the stairs to begin my laps, I could hear her speaking to someone with an upset tone in her voice.

The love and light definition is like a prayer made for the betterment of other people that you may want to help during their time of need. It can be verbal or through your mind. Whichever way, it reaches the angels and they in turn send it to the person in need.

Since I try to practice sending quiet prayers to others who seem in turmoil, I began asking my universe to send love and light to her heart to help her feel less pain. I practiced sending her joy and understanding to reach her heart and help change her mindset.

By sending others love and light, it is a powerful way of communicating positively to a friend or foe. In the process, the feelings of animosity vanish leaving only clear and absolute energy. It allows your heart to open letting the hurt and bad feelings leave while making your positive energy available for others.

Once you recognize your own need of receiving love and light, it becomes something to share. Through the journey of forgiveness, we can see how allowing our emotions to heal can open us up to the available space in which we can grow.

On this path of forgiveness, we can help ourselves along with others who are hurting. As we notice others are struggling with life's disappointments, we can use this practice to alleviate their pain. Since we experienced how the pain has subsided for us, as we send others love and light along with forgiveness, we know it to be true and can be life altering and affirming as well.

When we encounter others facing sadness, we offer our love and light in order to see them emerge from the darkness. It is probably one of the most powerful, yet easiest ways, to assist in changing those in our immediate world and even the world as a whole.

We all have friends and family who lost loved ones. By sending them love and light, you are sending positive energy to their heart. The more positive energy they receive, the more they can seem to handle the hard times. The more optimistic energy they receive, the more promising energy is able to be released from them.

Think of their heart as a bucket; the more you send them hopeful energy, the more their bucket is filled with positive vitality. For instance, when my father passed, the many notes, cards, and greetings filled my heart embracing the hurt. This practice of sending love and light is powerful. It only works when they are sent with the utmost good intentions for the other person's highest good.

Sending love and light is the perfect practice to continue on your journey. As you come along those on your path who have a different truth, send them your love and light. This unique practice not only fills their bucket but also fills yours. Its special power can take their pain away the same way it takes yours away. Simply have the best intention and watch as hearts all around you are filled with love and light.

49

Acknowledge the Gift of Your Labor

One day in the summer when I didn't have any tutoring, I packed a lunch and brought my favorite book to the beach to relax. While I sat reading, a small boy no more than 3 years old was wearing a bright yellow sun block shirt with his board shorts and having the best time walking with his dad to the water and back to their spot with wet sand. It brought a smile to my face with tons of memories flooding over me.

Being at the beach or the grocery store nowadays can bring lots of memories to mind. When this happens to you, enjoy the beautiful memory that comes to mind. Everything a mom does with and for her kids takes up a lot of time and energy. It is a funny thing how we only remember the fun times and not all the labor that was involved.

Be sure to acknowledge all the gifts of your labor. Both unnoticed and uncompensated labor for many years as a mom can take a toll. Think of all the work that nobody noticed and start giving yourself the acknowledgement you deserve. Remember that this was all essential to the function of your household and ultimately raising your kids to be the responsible and independent people they are now in our society. That is definitely something to be proud of and to celebrate.

As I walk upstairs in my home, I have a collection of Christmas poses from Target or JCPenney from the time when they were one and three to about middle school age. Also hanging on the wall are their college graduation pictures and a collage picture frame with them from every age on vacations or just around the house. I remember thinking about doing this when they were just babies. I wanted to have these pictures for me for the day when they were gone and living their own lives. It really is a treat to see these every day and it reminds me of all their cute smiles of different stages and all their accomplishments.

When you find yourself upset because your nest is empty, be sure to take a breath and remember that your labor helped that happen. As we rocked them to sleep in our arms, imagining them off on their own seemed so far off. Now we're thinking, "Where did all the time go?" Smile! You got them there! Enjoy the fruits of your labor!

There will definitely be days when you simply feel tired. Be sure to be kind to yourself and rest. Sit back and breathe while recalling all the large and small things you did for your children. Not only can you pat yourself on the back, but you can acknowledge all your hard work that helped get them out of the nest.

Now with both girls gone and married, I have updated pictures from their weddings and a group shot of all six of us from a vacation together. The group shot is hanging right in my living room to look at each day. While I work on my lesson plans for my tutoring or as I do my editing or writing for my books or blog, I'll stop and take a peek at them. Just seeing their faces in these photos brings such a feeling of love. It's like they're right here with me.

As I sit back and see how far I've come from raising my kids to my writing stage, I've always dreamt of doing this. I know I have used my gifts of labor as accomplishments. Since I've had to learn so many new things to become a self-publisher, I simply look back at all the things I accomplished when raising my kids and use that energy and self-confidence to get me through my next stage. Just think; all those crazy and funny days have led to this point.

Be sure to replace any sad thoughts with ones of those fun times. I don't know about you, but when I think of all the great times with my kids, I wouldn't give those up for anything. Now smile, big, bigger, from ear to ear! Say out loud, "I'm awesome!"

50

Enjoy Your New Stage

As you find yourself at this last chapter, I'm hoping your mind is filled and racing with all your new thoughts and ideas. Because my purpose of this book is to help parents enter this new stage with some positive tools, this is a great time to go back and review or dog-ear (I know some writers & librarians hate this!) the chapters that spoke to you.

Although you will feel sad from time to time because your child has flown the nest, be happy in the fact that they are out there learning and practicing to be an adult. Remember that they're doing it because of everything you've done. Enjoy the feeling of happiness as your child moves into their new apartment or through their college experience by continuing to be their supportive cheerleader.

I shared all my personal thoughts and ideas in each chapter. I can remember when each idea came to mind like the first day my kids took their first step. That's how big this moment is. It's definitely a different feeling because it is a whole new stage. You will feel happy, sad, somewhat depressed, and sometimes lost. And that's okay. It is really up to you to take control of the wheel and start living your new stage of life for you.

By all means, I am definitely not saying that feeling sad or lost is bad. You need to feel all your feelings. Let the tears roll out and let go of the sadness. Once you do that, you leave room for all your new ideas to come in and all your new adventures to happen.

Think back as you begin to live in this space and recall all the sacrifices you made. Everything you gave up has come back to you in a positive way. All that driving to their sporting events, to early study groups at school, and rushing from work stuck in traffic to support them has paid off.

I recall a text I received from my daughter who swam for her college. After an away swim meet, they stopped at a pizzeria and picked up pizza like normal. One of her teammates had a full blown meltdown because her slice was a bit burnt with a dough bubble. "Thanks for not raising me to be an idiot." Best text message ever.

I think the best 'thank you' that molded me for this stage was from my youngest. It wasn't just one but many from her thoughtful thank yous for everything I bought for her as she grew up from elementary to high school. Anytime we went grocery shopping, where she'd help me with the cereal or Gatorade special, she worked hard to organize the cart to make sure everything fit.

She was also the muscle that helped get all the bags into the house and into their spot. But most importantly, I always received a thank you. They always touched my heart. So every time I had to do extra work such as tutoring to make ends meet, I always had those thoughtful moments pinned to the back of my mind making my sacrifices worth it.

Those moments will come when you find tears making their way down your cheek. Simply flip through my book and look at one of the parts that fit what you're feeling at that time. Fill your heart with as much positive love & memories as possible and make a plan. Even making the plan helps soothe and calm your heart and soul.

Know that this book was written with love to help support you at this new stage in your life.

About the Author

Pilar is an educator of over 20 years. She watched her daughters reach their goals and follow their dreams as they played their sports in college. With her husband, they supported them by financing and attending their tournaments.

After living through the first 8 years as an empty nester, she wanted to help other moms and parents by sharing her strategies she used when her and her husband entered this new stage of life. She has returned to bike riding, fishing, and fulfilling her passion of writing books to help others.

Her first book is *Parenting Scholar Athletes*. She continues to write about Becoming an Empty Nester for Single Parents, for Adult Children, and for different stages that moms encounter such as Kindergarten, entering middle school, and attending high school.

Pilar lives with her husband in beautiful Encinitas, CA awaiting the next stage of becoming grandparents.

Many thanks for reading this book. If you have any questions, please feel free to contact me:

Email: pilar.regan@gmail.com

Twitter: @pilarkellenbarger

YouTube: https://www.youtube.com/channel/UCp_7yLTDKcCfTMTjMFtNyBQ

@pilarkellenbarger3912

Website: www.pilarkellenbarger.com

Bibliography

Asprey, Dave. "Deep Breathing Strengthens Your Brain and Boosts Attention Span, Says New Study." Dave Asprey Blog, 17 May 2018, blog.daveasprey.com/breathing-sharpens-brain-study/.

Miller MC. "Remembering as a form of therapy. Why reminiscing can be therapeutic." http://healthyliving.msn.com/health-wellness/remembering-as-a-form-of-therapy

Jones ED. "Reminiscence therapy for older women with depression. Effects of nursing intervention classification in assisted-living long-term care." J Gerontol Nurs. 2003;29(7):26–33.

Klever, Sandy. "Reminiscence Therapy: Finding Meaning in Memories: Nursing2020." LWW, Lippincott Williams & Wilkins, Inc, 2013, journals.lww.com/nursing/fulltext/2013/040 00/Reminiscence_therapy__Finding_meaning_in_memories.11.aspx.

Leardi, Jeanette. "How A Dose Of Nostalgia Could Boost Your Self-Esteem." HuffPost, HuffPost, 5 Oct. 2013, www.huffpost.com/entry/benefits-of-nostalgia_n_4031759

Mason, Peggy. "With a Little Help from Our Friends: How the Brain Processes Empathy." Cerebrum: the Dana Forum on Brain Science, The Dana Foundation, 1 Oct. 2014, www.ncbi.nlm.nih.gov/pmc/articles/PMC4445583/

Fisher, MD, James Keith, and Rebecca Stanborough. "Smiling with Your Eyes: What Exactly Is a Duchenne Smile?" Healthline, 2019, www.healthline.com/health/duchenne-smile

Jaffe, Eric. "The Psychological Study of Smiling." Association for Psychological Science - APS, 2011, www.psychologicalscience.org/observer/the-psychological-study-of-smiling

B, Osman. "5 Powerful Reasons Why Goal Setting Is Important." Code of Living, 14 Feb. 2020, www.codeofliving.com/blog/5-powerful-reasons-goal-setting-important

Fraga, Juli. "Friends Can Improve Your Health and Well-Being, Especially during the Holidays." The Washington Post, WP Company, 2 Dec. 2018, www.washingtonpost.com/national/health-science/friends-can-improve-your-health-and-well-being-especially-during-the-holidays/2018/11/30/e31fb31a-ecd0-11e8-baac-2a674e91502b_story.html

Smith, Sylvia. "How to Spend More Quality Time with Your Partner." Lifehack, Lifehack, 17 Oct. 2019, www.lifehack.org/articles/communication/10-ways-spend-more-quality-time-with-your-partner.html

Lewis, Benny. "How Adults Learn: 6 Important Things to Know." "Fluent in 3 Months - Language Hacking and Travel Tips", 26 Feb. 2019, www.fluentin3months.com/how-adults-learn/

Klosowski, Thorin. "The Science Behind How We Learn New Skills." Lifehacker, www.lifehacker.com/the-science-behind-how-we-learn-new-skills-908488422

Carver, Courtney. "Declutter and Downsize to Create a Life with Room for What Matters Most." Be More with Less, 18 Sept. 2014, www.bemorewithless.com/room/

Williams, Laura. "How to Declutter & Downsize Your Home Effectively – 9 Essential Tips." Money Crashers, 2015, www.moneycrashers.com/declutter-downsize-home-tips/

Kondo, Marie. The Life-Changing Magic of Tidying Up. Ten Speed Press, 2015.

Bertone, Holly. "Which Meditation Is Right For Me?" Healthline, 2017, www.healthline.com/health/mental-health/types-of-meditation

Young, Karen. "How Anxiety Interferes With Decision-Making –
And How to Stop It Intruding." Hey Sigmund, 2021, https://www.
heysigmund.com/

Cherry, Kendra. "How to Get out of a Rut." Very Well Mind, 10 Feb.
2022, https://www.verywellmind.com/

Lee, Kevan. "Your Brain on Dopamine: The Science of Motivation."
James Coleman, 9 Jan. 2014, https://lisarodriguezx.weebly.com/blog/
your-brain-on-dopamine-the-science-of-motivation.

Special thanks to Dr. Belynder Walia, Psychotherapist, for her beautiful cover testimonial and support.

Founder of Serene Lifestyles

Dr Belynder Walia www.serenelifestyles.com

OTHER TITLES BY PILAR KELLENBARGER

Parenting Scholar Athletes

Excerpt from:

Chapter 10: Coachable Through Positive Thoughts

Coachable Students Emulate Their Parents

Because our children are like sponges, they are aware of what we do and emulate those actions. We watched them do this as babies and now they are doing it as pre-teenagers. Since they will imitate our actions and thinking, it is vital to be the parent who models coachable qualities. Michael says, "My best skill was that I was coachable. I was a sponge and aggressive to learn." Coming from the king of coachable, his words are valuable to parents because they state what is in the mind of a successful athlete who is coachable.

If you show disrespect or quitting, those are the qualities your children may pick up. It's all about showing them their path towards success. Vince Lombardi, one of the greatest coaches in football and a national icon whose name is on the Super Bowl trophy, believed in an athlete's dedication and effort. He once stated, "Once you learn to quit, it becomes a habit." Another famous quote of his is, "The only place success comes before work is in the dictionary." As we can see, great players have the high qualities that a great coach is looking for.